THINK AGAIN

Discover Possibilities
Hidden in Plain Sight

OTHER BOOKS BY ROGER CRAWFORD

Playing from the Heart

How High Can You Bounce?

THINK AGAIN

Discover Possibilities
Hidden in Plain Sight

Roger Crawford

Thrive Publications
P.O. BOX 2336
Granite Bay, CA 95746
(800) 311-3344

THINK AGAIN

Thrive Publications
P.O. BOX 2336
Granite Bay, CA 95746
PHONE: (800) 311-3344, (916) 773-4455
FAX: (916) 797-3038
WEB: www.rogercrawford.com

Crawford, Roger;
2. Possibilities; 3. Tennis players - United States-Biography;
4. Physically handicapped-United States-Biography.

Cover: David Durham; Interior: Tim Chambers

Printed in the United States of America

ISBN 0-9779306-3-7

ACKNOWLEDGEMENTS

Although this is a book about possibilities, it is impossible to ad-equately acknowledge the inspiration and influence I have received from others. With heartfelt gratitude I would like to thank:

— MY AMAZING WIFE KATHRYN, who taught
  me that unconditional love is truly possible. I
  thank God every day for the blessing of you!

— OUR CHILDREN, who patiently endured my
  "motivational minute" around the breakfast table
  as you went off to school. I pray that you will enjoy
  a life brimming with abundant possibilities.

— MY COLLEAGUES IN SPEAKERS ROUNDTABLE.
  You all have been so unselfish with your knowledge and
  so generous with your encouragement. Thank you for
  walking with me during the challenges and celebrating
  the great joys. I cherish each and every one of you!

Acknowledgements continue on reverse…

— PASTOR RAY JOHNSTON, for being a
steadfast friend and spiritual mentor. My
sincere appreciation for teaching me to trust in
God's power, promises, and possibilities.

— ELEANOR DUGAN, for the ability to transform my
gibberish into coherent thought. This book would have
been impossible without your talent and commitment.

— MARK AND CELESTE CUELLAR, dear friends who
have brought love, laughter, and healing to our family.

— PATTY LAUTERJUNG, whose intellect, insight, and
quick wit were a great support in the birth of this book.

— OVER 4,000 AUDIENCES, who have given me
the unique privilege of sharing my message.

— AND ABOVE ALL, TO GOD for His never-
ending grace, amazing love, and humbling
acceptance of a flawed human being like me.
You are the Creator of all possibilities!

CONTENTS

INTRODUCTION   10

CLARIFY YOUR PURPOSE   18
  Define the Impossible   19
  Five Cliché Questions   23
  Who Can Do the Impossible?   33
  What's Your Philosophy About Possibilities?   37
  TiVo   41
  Seven Possibility-Busting Beliefs   45
  Watch Your Mouth   49
  Identify Your Possibility Zone   53
  Shooting Mosquitoes   57
  The Day My Finger Got Stuck   61
  No Legs to Stand On   63

IDENTIFY YOUR PESSIMISM   68
  Doing the Turkey Trot   69
  Pooh's View of Possibilities   71
  Fear versus Anxiety   77
  The "Go!" Technique   81
  Clean Your Closets   83
  The Language of Possibilities   87
  Blue Genes   91
  A Possibility In a Traffic Jam   95

Finding a Parking Space   97
Tasting the Hot Dogs   101
Chariots and Trumpets   103
The Phantom Garage Door   107

AMPLIFY YOUR POTENTIAL   112
The Parable of the Talents   113
What Are You Really Bad At?   117
It's Curtains   119
The Devil Made Me Say It   121
The Future Farmers Teach Me English   123
Eagles and Sloths   125
Sisters Cutting the Mustard   129
What's Behind a Name?   133
Ask, Connect, Persist   139
Six Degrees of Separation   143

MULTIPLY YOUR POSSIBILITIES   146
What Is a Possibility Partner?   147
Family and Friends: A Running Start   153
Watt's Up?   157
Bank On Your Possibilities   161
Standing Taller   165
What a Singing Pig Taught Me   169
Inspiring Confidence: Two Hands Working   171

Have You Kissed Your Ashtray Today?   175

Inspiring Employees   179

Strength In Numbers   183

QUANTIFY YOUR PROGRESS   188

The Power of (Im)possibility Thinking   189

"If I Ever Decide to Worry"   193

Hoping or Happening?   197

Don't Just Do Something—Sit There!   199

Act With Impact   201

Perfect Timing?   205

Patient? or Passive?   207

Where's Your Air?   211

Playing to Win   215

Be Like Mike   219

Be an Amateur   221

Dare to Give Up   225

Dream the Impossible Dream   227

INDEX   231

i

INTRODUCTION

Is your phone ringing?

I love ringing phones! You never know who will be on the other end. That day in June 2005, it was an unfamiliar female voice. "Roger, this is Nancy Baker. I'm the executive producer for *Larry King Live*. We'd like to have you on the show."

She explained that the theme was people who have done the "impossible" – who have overcome some seemingly insurmountable challenges and realized amazing opportunities. I felt honored that Larry King thought my story would serve as an inspiration.

I began life with what some would call a disability or handicap. My perspective is that I have an "inconvenience." Prior to my birth there was no indication that something might be wrong. When my parents held me for the first time, they were understandably shocked at my appearance. My arms are shorter than normal, and I have two fingers on my left hand and one on my right. When my daughter Alexa was very young, she described my hands this way: "Dad, you have a 'peace sign' on one hand and a 'thumbs up' on the other." It is the result of a rare genetic condition called ectrodactylism. My parents have no signs of this anomaly. In addition, my right leg is missing the fibula, and the foot has three toes. This is my "good leg." My left leg was twisted at the knee so severely I was unable to walk and navigated stairs as if I was participating in a bobsled race!

It was at this point in my life that my parents showed me the life-transforming power of *Thinking Again* about life's possibilities. Doctor after doctor told my parents that I would never walk, and a wheelchair or crutches seemed to be my only option. "It is out of the realm of possibility" they heard over and over. Yet, they turned discouragement into determination and expanded the realm of what was possible. This attitude led them to a doctor at Shrines Hospital in Chicago. After examining me, he informed my parents that by amputating my left leg and reconstructing my knee, potentially I might walk! That's all they needed to hear.

Whenever we choose to pursue potential possibilities, if rewards are significant then risk is present. I often wonder how different my life would be if my parents had chosen to focus on the obstacle instead of the opportunity. At the age of six, the surgery was successful, and I was able to run and play like other children. Today, with the stability of a prosthesis, I am able to walk without a noticeable limp.

My *thinking again* led to becoming an avid athlete. I played football, basketball, and found my passion when I stepped on a tennis court. My athletic possibilities were realized when I played Division I college tennis at Loyola Marymount University. You might be thinking, "Hey, you have one leg, half a foot, and a total of three fingers. How well do you play tennis?" In addition to being a fully-certified instructor with the United States Professional Tennis Association, I had the opportunity to play against John McEnroe. Please don't be overly impressed. What I learned from this match was that a positive attitude doesn't work every time... he beat me!

Now back to the show. The big evening at CNN came. Larry King was ill, but Nancy Grace from *Court TV* filled in. Her interview style was crisp and to the point. She immediately asked about my birth defect, and I described the challenges I faced growing up and how my parents insisted I see possibilities instead of limitations. They refused to let me feel sorry for myself. "I'm a lousy piano player," I admitted. "I had to accept that at a young age. But accepting the real impossibilities allowed me to focus on the possibilities instead of the problems."

For example, when I began playing tennis, I faced an obstacle. Because of my lack of fingers, I was unable to serve in the conventional way. Some well-meaning people suggested I abandon my dream of becoming a tennis player and try something more "realistic." But what a person sees as attainable is subjective and viewed through their prism of possibility. My coach said I could toss the ball up with two fingers, quickly grasp the racket with both hands, and swing through my serve. Initially I thought 'No way!' but my coach helped me *think again* about what was possible! My serve improved as I stayed inspired by focusing on it being possible! Today I have the best two-handed tennis serve in the world—I decided to overlook any impossibility that I might have the *only* two-handed serve in the world.

I said to Nancy, "My dad used to say, don't ask '*Am* I gifted?' Instead, continually ask, '*How* am I gifted?' I learned that I wasn't going to be the fastest or the most powerful tennis player because it wasn't in my strength zone. But I did possess the gift of patience. Therefore, if I hit the ball over the net one more time than my opponent, consistency could overcome power and speed and I'd win the point." Sharing my story on CNN was a blessing.

The morning after the interview, I started my workday as usual, turning on the computer to check e-mail. My mailbox was full! There were more than a hundred responses to my appearance, most of them from people eagerly telling me their own stories about how they too had done something that they had once thought impossible. The message their stories communicated was truly inspiring... they did what some said was impossible! *You can too!*

How do *you* respond to the ring of a telephone? Do you feel a little rush of exhilaration, wondering what is going to happen next? Or do you check caller ID to be sure it is someone you want to talk to? Or screen your calls with an answering machine? Or have someone else take messages so you're not bothered?

Think of a ringing phone as a metaphor for how eagerly you greet new and unexpected possibilities. Sure, it could be an annoying telemarketer, a bill collector, a tedious relative, a wrong number, or even an offensive caller. And, of course, you don't have to answer every time the phone rings, or agree to everything asked of you! But do you cut yourself off because you doubt your ability to deal with these possibilities? Do you fear that responding will just add another stressful demand to your already full plate? Is your life so closed that you've ruled out the possibility of something good at the other end of the line?

Of course, a metaphor comparing life's infinite possibilities with a ringing telephone can be carried only so far. No one should be a slave to interruptions and distractions. Life can be frittered away by jumping at every opportunity and leaping to accept every challenge without a clear vision of what's important to you.

I have read that a number of legendary VIPs have astonished callers by answering their own phones. They believe this immediate, direct contact creates more possibilities than the "protection" of an obstacle course of secretaries and assistants. And these same VIPs share another eccentricity: they have often achieved the impossible.

WHAT'S AHEAD?

So, one day you enthusiastically share a dream that you're passionate about. And your trusted listener smiles skeptically and says, "But is that possible?" Or they stridently say, "Who do you think you are?" These words can be discouraging and create self-doubt. My question for you: Is that negative mindset temporary? Do you rethink your objectives and decide your dream was just an idle fantasy?

Or do you marshal your inner resources and recommit yourself to your possibilities? That's why I wrote this book—to rekindle your motivation and expand your realm of possibility.

PREMISE:

You have greater possibilities in your life than you may imagine.

STRATEGY:

Uncover these possibilities by *thinking again* or thinking differently about your abilities and opportunities.

STEPS:

- Clarify Your Purpose

- Identify Your Pessimism

- Amplify Your Potential

- Multiply Your Possibilities

- Quantify Your Progress

I was on a radio program with author Jack Canfield, discussing the success of his *Chicken Soup for the Soul* books. He was asked, "How did you react when others said you couldn't make this happen?" Jack replied, "When everyone said it was impossible, I decided I needed to give myself a little extra time."

His story reminded me that we can achieve remarkable possibilities despite "impossible" circumstances. It requires perspective, purpose, and perseverance! And to *think again!*

1

CLARIFY
YOUR PURPOSE

What's impossible?

DEFINE THE IMPOSSIBLE

For various reasons, I will never be King of England, Miss America, or a Tsumo wrestler. You probably won't either. However, there are endless possibilities of what we *can* be! One of the best ways to open ourselves up to possibilities is to eliminate the truly impossible. That includes both things we really *can't* do and also things we really *don't want* to do. It is important to separate the two. If you have absolutely no interest in something, it doesn't matter how much talent you may have. Passion is crucial for achieving the impossible.

Let's start by deciding what's truly impossible. The maxim of the famous fictional detective Sherlock Holmes was that when you have excluded the impossible, whatever remains, however improbable, must be possible. Every one of us has thought something was impossible at some point and then done it. When I was a young boy, I thought tying my shoes was impossible because of having three fingers and shorter than normal arms. But a teacher inspired me to believe in possibilities by saying, "Failure only happens when you quit, Roger." I desperately needed this encouragement, and although it took me sixteen years, I finally tied my shoes. My feeling of accomplishment dulled when a new fashion trend appeared at school... Velcro shoes!

When it comes to speaking, it's impossible for me not to sweat. I was so nervous during my first paid speech that

I perspired through my suit. The audience members must have thought they were in the splash zone of an amusement park. Was it possible to overcome my nerves and stop sweating? No, and I still get nervous, so if you're in my audience, it may be best to sit near the back! A fellow speaker encouraged me to focus more on the audience and less on myself. When I embraced this mindset, accepted what was unchangeable, amazing possibilities opened up before me. Today it is crystal clear to me that my purpose is to encourage others.

The fact is, some things *are* impossible. Currently, time travel and living forever would be on that list, though new discoveries are being made all the time. Ending world hunger and curing cancer are vastly multifaceted tasks that probably require the efforts of more than one person. Thankfully, possibility thinkers inspired by a passionate purpose continue to pursue these and other lofty ambitions. Their achievements will change our world and help others *think again* about their possibilities.

What items are on *your* impossible list? Some people defeat themselves before they even try, based on their *perception* of their own possibilities. Perception can be a powerful dream-killer. Have you heard about the traditional elephant trainer's technique? Each baby elephant has a heavy chain put on its leg. No matter how hard it tugs, it can't escape. By the time the elephant is an adult, just a thin string serves the same purpose. The imprisoning chain is in the elephant's mind; its perception is that it can't escape. How many chains of impossibility do you have in your mind? How many are real, and how many are imagined?

To do the seemingly impossible, start by making a list of impossible things that you wish you could do. Get a sheet of paper and write down at least twenty things that you'd like to do but absolutely can't do. Once you get past the usual silly ideas like "give birth to a Porsche" and "fly to Mars without a spaceship," you'll notice that your answers start getting closer to home and to your heart. As your imagination soars, so will your awareness, until items start appearing on the paper that make you stop and *think again*. I'm willing to bet that you'll stare at some of the things you've written and realize that they are *not* impossible. With some ingenuity and effort, you will make them possible!

I can answer you in two words – im possible.

> — SAMUEL GOLDWYN
> HOLLYWOOD PRODUCER

FIVE CLICHÉ QUESTIONS

Before you can set out to see what's possible, you're going to need a direction, an intention, a *purpose*. The reason is "where we look determines where we end up." Here are some questions to help identify and clarify your purpose. You've heard some or all of them before, perhaps so often that they have become clichés. I'm going to ask you to consider them again—and then to answer some questions about your answers.

QUESTION 1. WHAT DO YOU WANT WRITTEN ON YOUR TOMBSTONE?
Does your answer indicate your definition of true success? Or is it someone else's?

This question usually evokes some emotion, as well as witticisms. Mine would say, "I'd rather be speaking!" A serious answer can help clarify our purpose. Powerful questions are what give our purpose power. When we think about the end of our lives, our legacy and hoped-for contributions come into focus. Did we realize our potential? Use our gifts? Do our best? Follow our dreams?

An interview I once read asked a similar question of people who had lived to be over a hundred: "How do you want to be remembered?" Their collective wisdom about what they hoped they had achieved was both insightful and inspirational. Their answers reminded me that understanding is not derived from experience alone. Wisdom is *experience evaluated*, a life examined.

The interviewer then asked them, "What would you have done differently if you could live those hundred years over again? What do you think you have not achieved?" Remarkably, most of their answers fell into four categories:

- "Give more."

- "Love more."

- "Risk more."

- "Be more."

What terrific philosophy for finding our purpose and realizing our possibilities! These are all passionate answers, and when passion aligns with purpose, it is easy to achieve the "impossible." An influential book of recent times is *The Purpose-Driven Life* by Pastor Rick Warren. I believe people respond so strongly to his ideas because we all want to live purposefully—to live a life that has meaning, significance, and substance. Too many people are led to believe that the purpose of life is to achieve prominence, which they translate as fame (or notoriety), wealth, and status. Yet, if they do achieve such prominence, they discover that it doesn't fulfill them. They are still hungry for meaning and contentment. They are forced to *think again*.

QUESTION 2. WHAT WOULD YOU DO
IF MONEY WERE NO OBJECT?

Do your answers describe what gives you joy? Or do some of them also address the things that give your life purpose? Do you see any connection between what gives you joy and what gives you purpose?

The news agent across the street from my friend's office has a big digital sign flashing the amount of the current lottery prize. Twice a week the number jumps if no one has won, and on those days more and more of her colleagues drift over to the window to check out the latest figure. When the amount tops $100 million, some slip out to buy tickets, either individually or as part of a pool. Then talk turns to what they'd do if they won the money. Being highly-educated, highly-paid professionals, their first thoughts are often of tax shelters and investments.

Then they discuss how their lives would be different. Here are some actual examples of their answers. (You might want to speculate on how successful you think each of these people would actually be in bettering their lives and achieving something meaningful).

- Austin would expand his lifestyle with material possessions, starting with a $1.3 million custom car. He has it all picked out. "A car says a lot about who you are," he says. (I don't know about you, but I have trouble visualizing where I would drive such a car without security guards jogging along beside each wheel, rather like the Presidential motorcade.) He's not sure $100 million would be enough money to maintain him for the rest of his life.

- Jack has always worked, while planning to be an independent entrepreneur like his dad. He's already parlayed a smart real estate investment and lots of sweat equity into a half-million dollars. "I'd like to start a luxury car dealership with my son and take my wife's side business national by selling franchises." He'd quit his job and put his lottery winnings into advancing his business plans more quickly.

- Jennifer would be happy winning a pool share of even a half-million dollars. "I'd reduce my lifestyle and take as much time off as possible to write novels full-time." She has already written several, all unpublished. If her winnings were sufficient, she'd like to live modestly in the south of France. She loves the process of writing more than she loves her current work, and she wouldn't mind being famous someday.

- Phillip says, "I'd use the money to fund orphanages back home in the Philippines, feed and educate poor children, and end poverty there." Typically, Filipinos send massive amounts of money home when working in the States. According to the website www.remithome.com this is one of the major sources of income in the Philippines. Think of the possibilities it is creating for others less fortunate.

- Maggie would pay for "college educations for my children, nieces, and nephews, then set each of them up with trust funds so they wouldn't have to work." She would continue to work because

she looks forward to the intellectual stimulation
and daily contact with her colleagues.

What would *you* do with a huge windfall? Would the tremendous responsibility be a blessing or a burden? How would you guard the money so it wouldn't slip away from you? How would you respond to the hundreds of people – friends, relatives, strangers, legitimate business people, and scurrilous con men – who would swarm all over you, so that you didn't dare answer the phone or step outside your house? What would change for the better in your life? And what would change for the worse? It's an interesting mental exercise.

The reality is that follow-up reports on people who have suddenly acquired a great deal of money indicate that few lived the life they had hoped for. The vast majority found their relationships with family and friends severely disrupted. Many subsequently divorced or were alienated from loved ones. They often abused drugs or alcohol and – ironically – went bankrupt. They weren't able to use the money to create their ideal lives or to fulfill long-held dreams. And they weren't able to enjoy what they won because they had no confidence thinking they would lose it all just as capriciously and be unable to regain it.

Think about this whenever you put your dreams and ambitions on hold, awaiting some stroke of luck. It may not take a huge windfall to finance a desired business project, educate yourself or your children, travel, improve your living situation, or fund a cause you care about. It may only require imagination, planning, enlisting the help of others, or a bit of patience. If you aren't waiting for someone or something outside of you to magically fulfill your needs and desires, you open yourself to noticing and creating possibilities that let you fulfill them *yourself*. And once you've created your own opportunities, then you believe you can do it again.

A common characteristic of people who await a huge stroke of luck to make their lives better is that, right or wrong, they don't see a direct connection between their efforts and their results. They reason that no matter how hard they work and how smart they are, they'll never get anywhere. They firmly believe that the only way to succeed is through the magic of a sudden bonanza. Enchanting fairytales of "pots of gold" are perfect illustrations of unexpected wealth. These stories led to the novels of the last century where the destitute hero or heroine was usually discovered to be the lost heir to a fortune. But in the twenty-first century, it is not a fairytale. The reality is most of us have the capacity and opportunities to make our own luck, shape our destinies, and create our *possibilities*.

In case you doubt the dangers of fantasizing about winning the lottery, people argue about the possibilities! Some employees have created pools to buy blocks of lottery tickets with the stipulation that all members would share the winnings equally. But what would happen if a pool member also bought a separate ticket that won? Would he or she also have to share those winnings? And what if someone who usually buys into a pool was out sick and didn't put any money in? Would the winners still give that person a share? What if someone lends someone else the money that buys a winning ticket? Would the lender then rate a percentage of that winner's share? These thorny questions have been raised and argued over, with people expending time and energy, taking sides until they quarrel. And all about imaginary money that no one has won!

QUESTION 3. WHAT WOULD YOU ATTEMPT IF YOU KNEW YOU COULD NOT FAIL?

Who would benefit if you did succeed? Is your project truly impossible right now – like "visit other galaxies?" If you could overcome doubt and fear, does your purpose suggest a course of action you could start right now?

British actor Harvey Jason was thinking about retiring after forty years as a character actor in movies and television but knew he'd need something to occupy his creative brain. While playing a dinosaur hunter in Steven Spielberg's *The Lost World: Jurassic Park*, he was inspired by a visit to a local bookstore in Eureka, California. As Jason was paying for his selections, the director himself wandered in. "Steven," Jason told him, "I've decided to open a bookstore!"

Jason didn't want to take unnecessary risks with his retirement money – and small general-interest bookstores are notoriously hazardous in the age of mega-stores and the Internet. Therefore, he decided to focus on the always popular mysteries and crime. Back in Los Angeles, he opened Mystery Pier Books. He soon added a section devoted to books that have been made into films, thus combining his twin passions. Jason's show-business connections brought many customers, and the shop has thrived for nearly a decade. Side by side you can find original editions of *The Postman Always Rings Twice*, *The Great Gatsby*, *East of Eden*, and a $40,000 set of *Harry Potter* books signed by J.K. Rowling. "Mystery Pier Books is like the most wonderful museum," says actor Michael Caine, "except that you get to keep the exhibits."

Of course, Harvey Jason took a risk, and he could have failed. Happily, he didn't. Success is never guaranteed, but sometimes we need to act as if it were.

QUESTION 4. WHAT IS YOUR GREATEST INSPIRATION?

*What motivates you? Who or what sets your
goals? What sparks your passion? And does
your passion support your current goals?*

It was twenty years ago, and there I was, about to listen to someone who had greatly influenced my life–Dr. Norman Vincent Peale. In my youth, a family friend had given me his book, *The Power of Positive Thinking*, and it inpacted my thinking about life's possibilities in a profound way. To share the speaking platform with this legend was one of the highlights of my speaking career.

Dr. Peale was in his nineties. His gait was unsteady, and he had difficulty walking up the stairs to the lectern. My initial concern was that perhaps he would not be able to finish his speech. Boy, was I wrong. All he needed was to grip the podium, steady himself, raise his right arm, and the magic began. It was as if he had found the Fountain of Youth as he mesmerized the audience with stories and uncommon wisdom.

"Positive thinking," he said, "is how you *think* about a problem. Enthusiasm is how you *feel* about a problem. The two together determine what you *do* about a problem."

Wow! Isn't that true of possibilities as well? If you *think* optimistically about a possibility and you *feel* passionately about that possibility, imagine what you can *do* about it. Think back to a time in your life when you felt most alive, most engaged, when you were *inspired*. Wouldn't you like to be able to re-experience that now?

Whether you think, in general, optimistically or pessimistically determines how you *think* about your possibilities. Your passion determines what you *feel* about your possibilities. Combine intellect and passion, and you'll discover what you can *do* with the possibilities all around you.

QUESTION 5. WHAT WOULD YOUR "PERFECT LIFE" LOOK LIKE?

What does your answer tell you about your values, your vision, and your relationships? How close are you now to perfection? What could you do to get closer to your ideal? What would you be willing to do to get closer to your ideal?

Recently, a TV talk-show host told viewers about her "Life List" of seven things she wanted to accomplish: "Be more patient. Take tennis lessons. Learn Spanish. Do more to help New Orleans. Learn to use a computer. Visit Amsterdam. Go to Africa." She invited viewers to create and act upon their own lists, an admirable activity for her and them.

I'm going to ask you to make a "Perfect Life List." When was the last time that you stopped to think about what *you* really want to do and be doing? What would you want to achieve if your life were perfect? Our planning time and energy are eaten up with figuring out the exhausting everyday intricacies of *living*, leaving little time for *life*. We're consumed with balancing work, family, bills, insurance, social obligations, education, money, schedules, and deadlines. If we manage to get 75 percent of all that done correctly, it is a triumph.

31

But every once in a while, we need to stop and think about the possible and the impossible. We need to make new mental connections and look for new directions. It's not that we can't do amazing things. It's just that often it doesn't occur to us to stop and take inventory of the amazing things we really want to do and then figure out a way to do them. Many people spend more time thinking about what to have for lunch than what to have for life. Make a regular date with yourself to plan a Perfect Life.

So, what do you think of your *answers* to these five questions? Do they reveal anything about your *purpose* in life? The possibilities you choose to notice and seize will be determined by how you see your future and your purpose.

It is not our abilities that show what
we truly are... it is our choices.

> — DUMBLEDORE
> *HARRY POTTER AND THE*
> *CHAMBER OF SECRETS*
> J.K. ROWLING

WHO CAN DO THE IMPOSSIBLE?

Over the years, I've discovered that people who can do the impossible – whatever their talents, skills, or backgrounds – have one thing in common: They all concentrate on what they *can* do instead of what they *can't* do. They focus on *possibilities* instead of problems.

Many of the recent leaps in technology have been achieved by mavericks who didn't believe in "impossible." Who would have been able to conceive of the enormous cultural influence of ideas like Craig's List, Google, Amazon. com, or eBay until someone risked the impossible? For example, what about the idea of being able to watch any movie you want, at any time you want, right in the comfort of your home? Impossible – or is it?

Some of you are old enough to remember when movies could be seen only in movie theatres, a time before video and DVDs. In the 1980s, new technology allowed home viewing, generating chains of rental stores, as well as late fees and occasional disappointment that the film you wanted to see was not in stock.

Then along came Reed Hastings, a former math major, Peace Corps volunteer, and software exec with a highly improbable idea. In 1998, he started an on-line video rental business called Netflix. It followed the traditional pay-per-rental model that included postage charges and late fees. The next year, Netflix started a monthly subscription concept. Then, with the introduction of lightweight DVDs, it became economically feasible to include postage in the fee. Since then, Netflix has built its reputation on having no due dates, late fees, shipping or handling fees, or per-title rental fees. It now offers more than 65,000 film and TV titles, and it had almost five million subscribers in 2006. What's next for Reed Hastings? Well, he'd like to send you *any* movie you want *whenever* you want it, using the Internet! The technological problems and legal complications will be enormous, and his rivals are all working as hard as they can to beat him to it. Many are saying his goal is impossible. But then, he's heard that before.

What about you? What prospects could you be overlooking? Between birth and adulthood, we use feedback from our culture, experiences, and those around us to build a mental image of our own capabilities and possibilities. This carefully-erected belief structure represents our place in society. It is our fortress and strength, the image we present to the world, but it can also become our prison. We operate within barriers that we've built ourselves, sometimes blocking access to exciting opportunities and possibilities.

To look past our protective structures and norms requires real bravery. *Possibilities* can be frightening. *Potential* means uncertainty, which is always uncomfortable. It is *so* much easier and more comfortable to go with the status quo, to do what is expected of us. It is so much trouble to have to *think again*.

Do you remember sitting in a math class, working out a problem written on the board? You were sure you had figured out the right answer. The teacher looked around the room, eyes moving from student to student, and then she called on *you*. What a great moment! Suppressing your excitement, you gave the answer. There was a pause while you waited for her congratulatory smile. Then you realized the teacher was shaking her head. "No, not quite right," she said encouragingly. "You can do it. Think again."

Peak performers stick up their hand, determined to try, even if they are wrong. And they carry that encouraging teacher with them every day, urging them to keep trying. Whenever they hear a voice muttering, "That's not possible–you'll never succeed–don't bother trying–better safe than sorry," they change the channel. They tune in a new voice, loud and clear, telling them over and over, "Think again!"

Do you need to change the voice inside your head? I guarantee the change will open up possibilities that lead to the "impossible."

The more you try, the more you triumph.

WHAT'S YOUR PHILOSOPHY ABOUT POSSIBILITIES?

I was traveling to a speaking engagement and suddenly broke my artificial leg. In half! I'm known as someone who has experience in overcoming adversity, but doing the bunny hop in front of 400 executives wasn't going to be pretty. The local 7-Eleven was out of limbs, so I phoned home to get a spare leg shipped to me. No answer. I phoned my neighbor Jerry, and as we were speaking, Dave, our neighborhood FedEx guy, rang Jerry's doorbell. As soon as Dave heard about my predicament, he went into action. Jerry used my spare key to retrieve a spare leg, and a few minutes later Dave had it boxed and on its way to me, 3,000 miles away. It absolutely, positively had to be there overnight and it *was*, arriving just in time for my 11 AM speech.

That's the power of being possibility-focused rather than problem-focused. And the power of building a business's reputation on doing the seemingly impossible. Imagine the thinking that went into figuring out how to get packages anywhere within the continental U.S. overnight – making the impossible possible.

You find what you look for. If you look for problems, boy, you find them! If you look for possibilities, there they are too. Every morning when we wake up, we have these two choices:

OPTION 1

> *"Life is a series of problems. We are either confront-*
> *ing one, going through one, or coming out of one."*

Of course, we all face difficulties. Big ones, little ones, funny ones, and really tragic ones. That's a given. However, there is another way to look at things.

OPTION 2

> *"Life is a series of possibilities. We are either approaching*
> *one, embracing and benefiting from one, or pursuing one."*

Which philosophy do you choose? Are you going to devote your energy to noticing your problems or your possibilities?

Let's start with how you would like to *feel*. Wouldn't you agree that being inspired by possibilities makes you feel energized, optimistic, and hopeful? And during the times when you lack hope, you tend to feel lethargic, disheartened, and unmotivated? In other words, when your perception of possibilities is positive, your self-esteem and performance are sky-high, but when your *perception* is pessimistic, they suffer.

Possibilities are rarely limited by our lack of talent, time, or training. It is our *perception* of our own limitations that holds us back. It is not aptitude or ability, but our *attitude* about our aptitude or ability that sabotages us. The greatest limits on what we can do, be, or achieve are the barriers we create ourselves. These barriers are incredibly powerful despite the fact that they are both invisible and imaginary. Our possibilities are constructed or destructed by our thoughts and attitudes.

Someone I consider a true possibility thinker is noted Christian author Chuck Swindoll. His philosophy on possibilities is well expressed in the following quote:

> The longer I live, the more I realize the impact of attitude on life. The remarkable thing is we have a choice every day regarding the attitude we will embrace for the day. I am convinced that life is ten percent what happens to me and 90 percent how I react to it. And so it is with you... we are in charge of our attitudes.

If you want to change your possibilities, *think again* about any erroneous beliefs you have about your abilities. All too often, we accept negative beliefs, even if we have little or no evidence to support this pessimistic view. Many people underestimate themselves and simultaneously overestimate others. Mistakenly, we feel that if others seem to be doing better than we are, they must be better than we are. We accept the false belief that we are incompetent, inadequate, or incapable of achieving greatness. How often do you perform better than you expect to? It almost never happens because you don't believe you can do any better. To unlock your possibilities, change the way you *think*.

If an elderly, but distinguished scientist says
that something is possible, he is almost
certainly right; but, if he says that it is
impossible, he is very probably wrong.

— ARTHUR C. CLARKE
BRITISH AUTHOR, INVENTOR

TIVO

When I was a young man, the thought of shaking hands with people nearly paralyzed me with anxiety. Because I have one finger on my right hand, I anticipated they would respond negatively. In my anxiety, I visualized people being visibly startled when they saw my hands, and I replayed this mental recording over and over. I TiVoed it.

Fortunately, my tennis coach, a very wise man, took me aside one day. "Roger," he told me, "you can never reach higher if you keep your hands in your pockets." He refocused my thoughts on possibilities instead of a perceived problem, giving me a whole new video to watch.

Both fear and possibility are strong motivators. When you are gripped by anxiety, you are anticipating a negative event. A good way to feed and reinforce this fearful mind-set is to TiVo your past failures, hurts, and disappointments. TiVo is an amazing technology that lets you record, replay, and even skip commercials while watching TV. Our mental TiVo works the same way, letting us re-experience a rejection, discouragement, or fear over and over again. When we decide to view new programming and uncover new possibilities, we may still hit the negative rewind button out of force of habit. Then, we end up reliving past negativity, thus creating a vicious cycle that sabotages access to new possibilities.

To break the cycle, use your mental TiVo to replay your past *successes* rather than your negative experiences. As you do, your courage will grow and your hope for your future will increase. You might ask, "Don't people who succeed have negative events in their past?" Of course, but they realize that they can live in anxiety or they can live in hope, based on what they choose to dwell on. They anticipate that their efforts will probably produce positive outcomes. They inspire and energize themselves with positive scenarios.

Have you ever stopped short of pursuing future possibilities because of a past experience? It's interesting that what sometimes discourages us from attempting the extraordinary can be something unchangeable in the past. Everything bright and wonderful that the future holds is shot down because of a long-ago disappointment. Let's *think again* about our history and reevaluate the meaning we place on it.

Here is a mental image that you may find empowering. Our past experiences are like a closet of old home movies—images filled with joys and jolts, hurts and heights. We all have a choice about which movies we choose to take out and rerun. If we dwell on the ones about failure, our energy wanes, negative expectations begin to dominate, and possibilities fade. If we replay the images about joy and courage, our confidence soars.

Of course, one of the intriguing things about looking at old images is how much our perspective has changed. The tree that seemed so huge is actually a tiny sapling. The same is true of disasters. Some events remain true tragedies, offering important life lessons and wisdom, but others now seem trivial, irrelevant, and even funny. Your past is defined by what you choose to dwell on. Don't let old negative images define your future!

Changing what you choose to focus on diminishes anxiety. Fear is hungry and needs food in the form of negative thoughts. Have you ever noticed that if you try to increase your energy and motivate yourself by using anxiety, you spend more time thinking about what can go wrong rather than how things can go right? Dwelling on potential pitfalls makes you act defensively. You expect the worst and over-react at any sign of failure. Concentrating on avoiding what you fear almost guarantees that it will happen. It's like someone telling you, "Be sure you don't drop that." Immediately, you're all thumbs.

People are either encouraged or discouraged by what they chose to dwell on from their past. They look for evidence to support their current mind-set. As they look into the future, they may glance back at past failures and use it as a template for future failures. However, the people who realize possibilities are those who identify possibilities in their past and use that experience as the framework for future possibilities. In the movie *Pee-wee's Big Adventure*, Pee-wee counsels a waitress who has "always wanted to visit France, but..." and she tells him all the reasons why this is impossible. "Everyone has a big 'but,'" he warns, and persuades her to follow her dream.

Remember the opening sequence of the classic Dick Van Dyke Show? Every episode, behind the credits, he'd walk in his front door as the lively theme song played. Half the time he would fall kersplat over the ottoman, and half the time he'd spot it and nimbly dance around it. You never knew which version you were going to see.

Now imagine running your *own* disaster on your TiVo, taking a huge pratfall over an obstacle. Then, switch the tape

43

and see yourself stepping around it at the last minute, giving a big, triumphant grin like Dick Van Dyke did. Choose to run that new tape, not the old one, and see yourself not failing but *succeeding*. Don't let your past hold you back. TiVo your successes and watch your possibilities grow!

Is a big "but" holding you back? Exercise your imagination to reduce your but.

SEVEN POSSIBILITY-BUSTING BELIEFS

While you're choosing a philosophy and a way to describe your life, start choosing to challenge some of the common negative beliefs that can keep you from seeing your possibilities. Seven beliefs that can definitely inhibit your success in life are:

1. *Accentuate the negative.* You may remember the old Harold Arlen/Johnny Mercer song, "Ac-Cent-Tchu-Ate the Positive, E-Lim-Mi-Nate the Negative." Our possibilities are infinite when we accentuate the positive, but very limited when we dwell on the negative. To counteract negative thought habits, identify a pessimistic viewpoint. Then gather evidence to support a contrary positive view. (If you need help, Chapter 2 describes a special kind of friend who can provide that positive perspective.)

2. *Blame yourself.* Here is a thought to embrace. We are not responsible for everything that happens. However, we *are* responsible for how we respond to everything that happens. Possibility thinkers are clear about what they can control and what they can't control. Why devote energy to things you absolutely cannot control or change? Focus on facts, not fault.

3. *Be inflexible.* "If I keep an open mind, my brain might fall out!" If we are rigid in our thinking, we limit our potential. Have you ever said, "Why didn't I think of that?" Perhaps those who did have developed the habit of searching for new and different ways of thinking and doing things. They identify exciting new options and are not limited by a fear of failure.

4. *Be your own severest critic.* Remember the schoolyard chant, "Sticks and stones may break my bones, but names will never hurt me"? I don't buy that. Negative names break your spirit and decrease your possibilities. And far worse than the bully down the street is your own inner persecutor who can really defeat you. If you hear a voice saying "Boy, you blew it again," or "You're the biggest idiot in the world," *think again!* Dr. Robert Shuller says, "Do not put yourself down; there are plenty of other people happy to do that for you."

5. *Believe things won't change.* When I was in high school, the song that everyone wanted to slow-dance to was "Always and Forever." It's a beautiful song, but the lyrics are just wishful thinking. Nothing stays the same. Yet, I have met people who crush their possibilities with the belief that "I'll always be this bad," or "Things will never get better," or "Everything always goes wrong," or "Nothing ever goes right." The truth is that everything changes. Life can be very different today and tomorrow than it was yesterday, so why can't it be a lot better?

6. Use Blue-Light Special thinking. One discount store uses a flashing blue light to signify a big discount. Some people discount their own abilities and accomplishments with similar emphasis, talking themselves down while exaggerating their liabilities and flaws. The negative is given priority over the positive. A typical response to an impressive achievement is dismissive: "It was plain luck. Anyone could have done it. Right place, right time." That's a sure way to limit possibilities. Put this advertising razzle-dazzle into promoting, not demeaning.

7. Predict a negative outcome. Have you met people who are convinced they can predict negative events in their lives? "Why try?" they ask. "I'll fall flat on my face again." Their pessimistic predictions rarely extend to foreseeing exciting possibilities and positive outcomes. Yet, no one is omnipotent. Baseball manager Yogi Berra used to say, "Predicting is hard, especially when it comes to the future." So, get rid of cracked and cloudy crystal balls. Instead, anticipate a positive outcome. This is the first step in achieving possibilities.

I've always believed that you can think positive just as well as you can think negative.

— JAMES A. BALDWIN
AUTHOR

47

WATCH YOUR MOUTH

"If thought corrupts language," wrote noted novelist George Orwell, "language can also corrupt thought." Words are more powerful than armies. There are lots of words that society uses to label actions in an attempt to influence behavior; words like *polite, civilized, manly, ladylike, honorable, high class,* and also their negative counterparts.

We can influence our own actions, positively and negatively, by how we refer to things and how we talk to ourselves. Here are some words and phrases to avoid. Stop yourself if you start to use them.

POSSIBILITY-SABOTAGING WORDS AND PHRASES:

> *Should*: I should have done better.
> I should be smarter than that.

> *Must*: I must not make a mistake.
> I must be an idiot.

> *Always*: That stuff always happens.
> It's always going to be this way.

> *Never*: I never get it right.
> I could never do that.

Now, reframe your words. The language of possibilities is encouraging and fortifies our perseverance.

POSSIBILITY-SUPPORTING WORDS AND PHRASES:

Could: I could try that.
That could be a solution.

Might: This might work.
I might win.

Often: Things often turn out okay.
I'm often on target.

Sometimes: That sometimes happens.
Sometimes I don't get it right.

When you catch yourself TiVo-ing a negative phrase, try restating it in more positive language. If this seems too uncomfortable and unfamiliar, consider at least setting a "statute of limitations" on old negativity. I got this idea from an organizational consultant who came to my office to help me be more organized, and therefore more effective. One thing the consultant advised was setting a "statute of limitations" on unread books, magazines, brochures, and catalogues, and all those old clippings I had intended to follow up on.

Wow, what an idea! Why not also put a "statute of limitations" on your worries and anxieties?

I remember thinking, "If I get rid of everything that I haven't gotten around to doing, will I have anything left to do?" Hanging on to old worries involves a similar lack of logic. People are afraid to let go of their worries, wondering, "Will I have anything else to think about?"

Let's say that someone close to you didn't approve of your choice when you started on some venture. Perhaps they felt it was too risky for you, or they were jealous or fearful that you might surpass them. Since then, you've done very well, but you continue to feel bad about that lack of support. Is it somehow disloyal to really succeed? Or, alternatively, will the negative prediction prove to be right and you'll soon crash and fall on your face? This double-pronged worry occupies your mind, sapping your energy and enthusiasm, while keeping you from noticing exciting new possibilities right under your nose!

Declare a moratorium. After a certain point, these worries are past their "sell-by" date. Just like other obsolete stuff cluttering your closet, pack them up and get rid of them. If that's too uncomfortable at first, set aside one minute every day to focus on that obsolete worry. You'll still have 1,439 minutes left in the day to *think again* about possibilities!

Man does not live by words alone, despite the fact that sometimes he has to eat them.

— ADLAI STEVENSON
AMERICAN POLITICIAN

IDENTIFY YOUR POSSIBILITY ZONE

"Hey, Dad, you're phat!" The first time I heard my kids say that, I wanted to ground them for life. I sucked in my gut, straightened my shoulders, and held my breath. As soon as I had regained consciousness, I noticed their laughter was mixed with admiring looks. They explained that "phat" refers to fab, not flab.

So here's a thought. Are your possibilities phat? Do they stir your passion and challenge your talents and abilities? Are they just within your perceived realm of possibility? Are you expanding that realm? "Good enough" gets in the way of great possibilities. Of course, we all need goals that are attainable, measurable, and achievable. They build strength, confidence, and positive expectations. But extraordinary possibilities require lofty thinking and imagination.

What about *you*? Are you starting to see a pattern of how to use your resources, talents, and passions to achieve the possible and attempt the "impossible"?

POSSIBLE-SELF EXERCISE NO. 1:

- What are your favorite things to do? What do you do best? (They're not necessarily the same things.)

53

- What do you dislike doing or usually procrastinate about?

- What are you so bad at, that when you try, it is often a disaster? (Are you really that bad, or have you decided to prove to others that you can't do this so they won't expect you to?)

- What do *other* people see as your greatest strengths? As your greatest weaknesses?

- Is there something specific you'd like to attempt? What will it take to achieve it?

- What do you already have? What are you missing?

- Can you leverage your weaknesses to turn them into strengths? Can you subcontract the missing factors? Can you involve others in supplying what's absent? Can you redesign your strategy to eliminate the need for anything you can't deliver?

Fantasizing about your "possible self" can help you identify the qualities that you'd be willing to defend, those you'd like to develop, and those you'd like to get rid of. The images you create as you do this can clarify your values and provide powerful stores of resilience. Most of all, you'll start to notice more options.

What is your ideal "possible self?" In an experiment at the University of Texas, 173 adults, aged 18 to 86, were asked to describe their hoped-for possible self (for example, *glamor-*

ous, powerful, esteemed) and also their feared possible self (*unwanted, out-of-shape, lacking control*). As expected, researchers Susan Cross and Hazel Markus found big expectation differences between those who had previously scored high in rating their life satisfaction and those who had low scores. There were also differences by age group.

POSSIBLE-SELF EXERCISE NO. 2:

Relax and think of the self you'd like to *be*. Jot down your description. Then do the opposite, concentrating on the negativity and listing what you fear becoming. Did this exercise offer you clearer ideas about what you want to accomplish?

Shakespeare has Hamlet say, "There is nothing either good or bad, but thinking makes it so." Concentrate on how your life is and how it could be. If you waste time looking back at what it wasn't, you're not noticing the new opportunities all around you. It's an extraordinarily simple concept but extraordinarily difficult for some people to act on.

What in life have you achieved by accident? Yes, there are wonderful instances of serendipity–stumbling across something delightful and unexpected. That's what makes each day a joyous adventure. However, whatever your objectives have been–learning to walk, read, drive a car, or use the newest digital device–chances are that you saw yourself achieving them, you intended to achieve, and you were willing to put time and effort into these goals.

So, once again, *identify your possibility zone*. Work within your strengths. There is a difference between your talents and your strengths. Talents are your inborn gifts and abilities–*what* you do well. Strengths are qualities like courage,

55

hope, resilience, and integrity—*how* you do well. Talents without strengths are like rocket ships without fuel; they won't get off the ground and soar.

Where you aim determines what you hit; as the popular saying goes, "shoot for the moon." Then, if you miss, the stars aren't bad as a backup. Even if you end up hitting your own foot (as I often do), at least you've activated your launch equipment.

Your focus is most often dictated by your beliefs and opinions of yourself. The importance of your perceptions of your own courage and competence cannot be underestimated. Faulty judgment can stop you before you start. What you see in yourself is what you get out of yourself! Focus on your unique skills and interests, and don't settle for anything less than the best possible you.

Decide how. Do it now.

SHOOTING MOSQUITOES

I will never forget the day I learned that my mother-in-law, Judy Allen Young, is a Hall of Fame member. Not for science or baseball or rock-and-roll. She is in the National Skeet Shooting Hall of Fame for her remarkable accuracy with a shotgun.

Now, I don't want you to have any misconceptions about the significance of this honor. Skeet shooting is not a casual gun sport like the shooting gallery at a county fair. It requires some serious shooting ability. I once asked Judy what she did to perfect her marksmanship.

She kiddingly replied, "We used to shoot mosquitoes for target practice." With her answer in mind, I understood just how skilled she was with a firearm. Let me put it another way: Since that day, I have not uttered another mother-in-law joke.

I was intrigued by her champion achievement and asked Judy to share some of her techniques of sporting excellence with me. Her response came to her with familiar ease, as though she were introducing me to an old friend. Her answers held remarkable insight as principles for life, whether on or off the skeet field. Here is what she said:

- Be ready when you call for your target. (Be fully prepared and focused. Then, just do it!)

- You can't shoot two targets at once. (Give it your full attention. Multi-tasking is much overrated.)

- Keep your cheek to the stock and follow through. (Stay steady and stay with it! Otherwise, none of the rest of it will work.)

So, the moral of the story? You can do lots of wonderful things in life. But if you don't fully *prepare*, keep your *focus*, and *follow through*, nothing great is likely to happen.

Here are some more thoughts on Judy's techniques:

Preparation: Success happens when extraordinary preparation meets extraordinary possibility. Have you ever heard someone say, "It was a good opportunity, but I wasn't ready"? The fact is that we are always prepared–either we're prepared to succeed or we're prepared to fail. Some convince themselves that they are unworthy or incapable of achieving their best. Then, when possibility presents itself, their mental conditioning prepares them for failure.

Focus: Here's an example of focus. It happened during a five-man-team skeet shooting competition in Bakersfield, California. The championship team was nearly finished with their event when they heard a roar go up from the crowd. Did they pause? No! Despite this noisy distraction, they pressed on, focusing intently on each target as it was called for and successfully broken. They continued their concentration, one target at a time. Then, as the team finished their event, they were surrounded by an exuberant crowd of spectators. The officials informed them that even before they were finished, it had become obvious they were probably going to win–not only the competition, but a new world record. Imagine if their concentration had wavered, and they had missed some of those shots.

Follow Through: All the preparation and focus in the world won't let us achieve our goals unless we actually follow through with our plans. We can have super skills, fine training, great ideas, and a clear vision of where we want to end up. However, if we don't take the necessary steps to get there – whether it's just a short-term project or a day-in, day-out marathon effort towards a long-term goal–then we will never be able to turn our possibilities into reality. There is a saying tennis coaches use to emphasize the importance of finishing your stroke. "Failure follows those who fail to follow through." True on the court as well as off.

I am convinced that possibilities are available to everyone. However, the people who realize possibilities are ready when they identify their "target." They are prepared mentally, physically, and perhaps spiritually when they pull the trigger. They focus, and they *follow through*.

Success in our own personal world-records is much like this. Stay focused on the target, and ignore the distractions. Great things will happen if you can just hit and break the next target, then the next. That's how a possibility life is. We achieve our purpose one target at a time.

If you aim for nothing, you'll hit it every time.

— AUTHOR UNKNOWN

THE DAY MY FINGER GOT STUCK

The passion that totally changed my life was tennis. It wasn't an obvious choice. In all likelihood my parents could never have predicted I had any potential in sports, given my physical challenges.

When I was twelve, my family moved from Ohio to northern California. By chance, our new home was across the street from the Greenbrook Racquet Club. The first summer we were there, I spent many hours sitting on a hill above the courts, watching people play tennis. There was something exhilarating about watching that ball thwack against their racquets and soar over the net.

One day I was in the garage and came across my Dad's old wooden tennis racquet. It was heavy and cumbersome, and I had a hard time holding onto it. Undaunted, I bought some tennis balls and began trying to hit them against the large, green backboard at the end of the courts. I experimented with several ways to hold the racquet before I found a technique that worked for me; the same way I hold it today. I'd pin the grip of the racquet to my right elbow with my left hand. However, I couldn't always hold the heavy wooden neck of the racquet with my right hand. When I swung hard, the racquet sometimes went flying. That explains why I had very few doubles partners back in those early days.

Then one day the local tennis shop got a shipment of the new Wilson T-2000 metal racquets. Two parallel bars connected the face of the racquet with the handle. I picked one up, and my finger accidentally slipped down between the two bars and got stuck. Instinctively, I tried to pull the racquet off, but it was snugly stuck to my finger. "I can hold this racquet!" I shouted, swinging it harder and harder. The racquet didn't budge.

My life had changed forever. I went on to become an athlete, a four-year high school letterman in tennis with a 47-win/6-loss record. At Loyola Marymount University in Los Angeles, I competed in NCAA Division I and earned full certification as a tennis coach through the United States Professional Tennis Association. My passion became my profession, and it opened a whole new world for me. Anything became possible!

Our passion determines what and how we feel about our own potential. Our ability to perceive possibilities expands enormously when we can identify both the value and *fun* of our objectives. *Value* is an intellectual concept. *Fun* is an emotion—a burst of child-like wonder and joy. The combination results in *passion*, an infinite energy source that can inspire us to tackle any obstacle in our path.

Think about the last time you felt totally fulfilled, when you knew that life just couldn't get any better. What were you doing? Probably it was something you are passionate about, something that you could and should incorporate into your life plan.

Passion + Purpose = Potential

NO LEGS TO STAND ON

Here's something you don't see every day. Two kids in an amusement park, running happily through the crowd, while holding ice cream cones, stuffed animals, and a pair of adult-size prosthetic legs. It was one of those zany events that regularly enliven the lives of people who discover possibilities – and everyone around them.

Dan Adragna was a high-level electrician foreman in Aptos, California, and an active single dad with two teenagers. One Christmas eve, he felt flu-like symptoms that grew so intense that he began to lose consciousness. He was rushed to Dominican Hospital in Santa Cruz, where he went into a coma. Dan had developed *septicemia* (blood poisoning), possibly from all the small wire cuts he routinely sustained on his job. The bacteria attacked his limbs. He lost parts of his fingers, and eventually his legs were amputated at the knee to stop the spread of gangrene. In the coming weeks, his heart flat-lined twice, and his family prepared for the worst. The next time he opened his eyes, it was February 10. He now weighed 85 pounds and was unrecognizable to his friends.

Dan spent the next four months enduring agonizing rehab. In the past he had been able to run with his kids. Now he was in a manual wheelchair. Almost a year after his near-death experience, Dan finally took his first step on two prosthetic legs. His mode of transportation was upgraded from wheelchair to an automobile with hand controls. He couldn't return to his former profession because he'd lost his dexterity and balance. You might be thinking that his potential was now limited. *Think again.*

Dan decided he now had the opportunity to help others discover their own possibilities in spite of their obstacles. One thing he did was volunteer to work with the teen ministry at his church. The teenagers' boundless energy inspired him, and the kids related to his strong sense of humor. Sure, he walked with a rolling gait, but they assumed he was just "strutting his stuff." Most were unaware of Dan's prosthetic legs – until the group trip to Great America.

The big day dawned, the buses pulled up, and several dozen excited kids exploded through the gates of the San Jose amusement park with chaperone Dan in hot pursuit. The students soon made a beeline to Invertigo, a double-inverted sidewinder, regarded as the mother of all roller coasters – ninety seconds of sheer hell, and thus irresistible. The kids nicknamed it "Barf-igo," because its high-speed loops and steep plunges sometimes have riders upside-down 138 feet up in the air. Each seat holds two, and some of the teens later claimed temporary hearing loss due to the hysterical screaming of their partners.

Dan courageously volunteered to go on the ride. He counted off the group and calculated that his partner in terror would be a shy 13-year-old girl. When it was Dan's turn to be strapped into a seat, he discovered, to his horror, that there were no leg supports. His legs just dangled. What would a G-force of five gravities do to his prosthetic legs? He didn't have time to wonder long. The ride took off!

The initial 138-foot lift and drop was completed without incident, and Dan breathed a sigh of relief. Then the inverted sidewinders began. Dan grabbed his knees, but his strength was no match for the G-force. The first leg to break free was the right one. But instead of flying off, the prosthesis started spinning like a shot-putter winding up before a launch, its toe rotating within inches of his partner's face. Alarmed, he reached over to protect her and loosened the grip on his left leg. It joined the first in rapid rotation.

The right leg reached launch speed and shot off like a rocket, sailing over the crowd below and vanishing. Seconds later, it was followed by the left leg. Dan glanced over at his 13-year-old friend, fearing she would be terrified. Instead, he saw her laughing uncontrollably. As the G-force continued, her face acquired the wrinkled look of one of those Shar-Pei dogs, and his own must have too, because she kept pointing at his face and laughing even harder.

A number of the students had witnessed the blastoff. As soon as the ride stopped, they scattered on a mission to find Dan's legs. Dan suddenly realized that he was stuck. He couldn't leave the ride without his legs. He suddenly had a terrifying vision of himself riding Barf-igo over and over until the park closed. Then he saw one of the most welcome sights he'd ever experienced. Two members of his youth group were running toward him, holding those cones, stuffed animals—and his precious legs. Everyone, including Dan, cheered!

Dan continues his quest to inspire others to uncover possibilities. Today, he is a key leader in Wheels for the World, an organization that finds wheelchairs for disadvantaged people throughout the world. He has traveled to many countries, encouraging others to see what's possible. When I told him about the concept of this book, he smiled. "When someone can go from crawling, or being carried, to the independence of a wheelchair," he explained, "they are transformed instantly. Independent mobility changes a person's thinking. It changes what's possible and that reveals new purpose."

The people Dan meets through his new job aren't the only ones who find new purpose. It was through attending a function to publicize Wheels of the World that Dan met, fell in love with, and married his wife Melinda. Their lives have never been the same and their future filled with endless possibilities.

Dan has made an unforgettable impact on my life! Some people love to show off their new outfit; Dan and I enjoy showing off our new legs. He inspires me to embrace my possibilities and live life to the fullest. The greatest lesson his life has taught me is problems don't reduce potential, they *reveal* potential.

Problems are only opportunities in work clothes.

— HENRY J. KAISER
KNOWN AS THE FATHER OF MODERN
AMERICAN SHIPBUILDING

2 IDENTIFY YOUR PESSIMISM

Why is it impossible?

DOING THE TURKEY TROT

One Thanksgiving, my daughter Alexa thought it would be a fabulous idea to run a 10K fund-raising race called the Turkey Trot. The proceeds provided meals for low-income families. I embraced the idea enthusiastically, and we both signed up. To ensure that I would not be the last turkey to finish the race, I started training daily. But after a couple of weeks, my bright self-image as a tireless young champion athlete began to fade a bit. My motivation began to lapse as I visualized the effort it was going to take.

Finally, I explained to my daughter that my schedule was so busy that perhaps we should delay our trot until the following year. Alexa, then eleven, gave me one of those reproachful daughter looks. "Dad," she chided, "you're focusing on the obstacles instead of the objective."

Huh? That sounded familiar. I'd been telling audiences that for years! There I was, dwelling on the daunting task ahead, instead of the exultation of crossing the finish line with my darling daughter.

I'm not suggesting that you discount the effort or difficulties involved as you pursue your possibilities. Don't kid yourself that an ambitious goal won't be tough. That's delusional thinking, and you'll soon lose momentum. Acknowledge up front how much work it's going to be, and you'll *increase* your possibilities instead of decreasing them. Anyone who makes it to the top (or to the finish line) understands the effort required to achieve desired possibilities.

A realistic assessment of the challenges ahead is not an adequate reason to abandon the race. Some people focus on the barriers they may face and abandon possibilities before they even begin. Those who make it—who even achieve greatness—are those who decide to take the first step anyway. And then the next... and the next!

Of *course*, there will still be disappointment, difficulty, and discouragement. How do we counteract that? My friend Jeff Salz, an accomplished rock climber, tells me that when his arms tire, he immediately thinks of the potential view awaiting him at the top. How about you? Have you thought of what your view will look like?

I am happy to report that I did not finish last in the Turkey Trot race. There was one person behind me, nipping at my heels: an athletic-looking young man, perhaps twenty-five years old. He was driving a golf cart, weaving back and forth to pick up the orange cones that outlined the racecourse!

The reality is that in the pursuit of ambitious possibilities, we are likely to fail or finish last. To stay optimistic we must *think again* about these experiences. Some people see setbacks as absolute failures, while others view them as important information gathering. If you are reluctant to attempt something because you fear negative results, here is a compelling thought:

Who really loses? The person finishing last or the one who never entered the race?

POOH'S VIEW OF POSSIBILITIES

The stories we read as children – and read to our children – often contain powerful messages about possibilities. Remember *The Little Engine That Could*? What a great parable about determination. How about Dr. Seuss's *Oh, the Places You'll Go!*, a story that rejoices in the potential everyone has to fulfill their wildest dreams? It's too bad this childhood wisdom sometimes fades as we age and become "terminally adult."

One classic character who lives a life filled with possibilities is A.A. Milne's Winnie-the-Pooh. What a great role model! Now, you may scoff and think, "What can I possibly learn from a storybook bear who loves honey?" Here's what.

Pooh is someone who refuses to become discouraged, despite dire circumstances and some pessimistic friends. In addition to level-headed Christopher Robin and bouncy Tigger, Pooh also has some fairly dispiriting pals. There's Eeyore, the dismal donkey, who walks around in a cloud of perpetual gloom and melancholy. And then there's worried little Piglet, always asking, "What if we're lost?" or "What if we fail?" It is up to Pooh to provide a positive alternate view.

One day, Pooh and Piglet are walking through the forest in a heavy wind that turns into a roaring gale. Piglet, as usual, becomes alarmed at the negative possibilities. "Supposing a tree fell down when we were underneath it?" Pooh thinks carefully. "Supposing it didn't?" he replies.

Pooh is always asking questions that challenge Piglet to think about circumstances from a different perspective. Pooh is helping Piglet to *think again*.

No matter who we are or what we have achieved, we all have a little Pooh and a little Piglet in us. People who are open to possibilities are focusing on their Pooh side. When we keep a little Pooh in our outlook, our possibilities multiply. If you constantly interpret situations and facts in Piglet mode, stop and consider the Pooh view. To be our best we all need to be full of Pooh. (Happily, people are constantly telling me that I am full of it.)

Have you noticed that many worries tend to fall into two categories—those that are unlikely and those that are unimportant? If paralyzing worry is blocking possibilities, try asking yourself these three questions:

QUESTION 1: HOW LIKELY IS THIS TO HAPPEN?

The reality is that almost anything *can* happen, but what are the *actual* chances? Like Pooh, question the probability of a negative outcome by considering facts. Facts build fortitude.

Some people seek out or invent drama to energize themselves. However, if catastrophizing has the opposite effect—if the imaginary possibilities for disaster distract you from the real possibilities for opportunity—go Pooh. Examine the facts, re-evaluate your thinking, and consider adopting an optimistic perspective.

Sometimes people come up to talk to me after my presentations. Occasionally, some tell me how they wish they could have my attitude, but it's just not possible. I am humbled by their comments, but in reality my life is not very different from theirs. We all face challenges and we all have choices. As we chat, it usually becomes clear that what's getting them down hasn't happened yet. In fact, there is often overwhelming evidence that it will probably never happen. They've been blinded by their personal viewpoint and haven't examined the evidence from an alternate perspective.

If you are stuck in Piglet mode, surrounded by alarming consequences that are blocking your way, seek out a Pooh. Not someone who offers empty platitudes of reassurance, but someone who can help you evaluate whether your thinking fits the facts. Maybe you're right. Maybe something *is* really wrong that needs to be confronted. Or maybe you're wrong. The French essayist Montaigne said, "My life has been a series of catastrophes—most of which never happened."

QUESTION 2: IF IT HAPPENS, IS IT REALLY IMPORTANT?

The main problem with focusing on problems is that they distract you from noticing and pursuing opportunities. One common piece of advice about unproductive worrying is: "You won't remember this worry in a hundred years." Hey, I think; I can't remember what I had for *lunch*, and I'm still at the table staring at my empty plate!

My late friend Richard Carlson wrote the book *Don't Sweat the Small Stuff*. What a profound life principle—to live positively and conserve your mental energy for possibilities instead of problems. As an objective self-observer, I realize that I have given disproportionate significance to the small stuff. Have you ever lain awake at night, worrying about something that *might* happen? The next morning you wake up and, momentarily, you've forgotten all about it. Then it comes back to you, and you say to yourself, "Time to start worrying again."

I find it fascinating that many people cope more effectively with the big stuff than the small stuff. Then they proceed to let little irritants assume insurmountable importance.

QUESTION 3: WHAT'S THE BEST THING THAT COULD HAPPEN?

Many self-help books advise the following way to increase your courage in tough situations: "Just imagine the *worst* that could possibly happen." The underlying logic is that this will strengthen you for whatever is to come. However, whenever I mention this strategy to people who are discouraged, they tell me they've already rehearsed and anticipated all the negative events so thoroughly that they can recite every tiny detail as if it had already happened.

Instead, my suggestion is to rehearse and imagine the *best* that can happen. Here's a positive strategy. Let's say you are considering pursuing a possibility that seems a bit daunting. Therefore, to prepare for the great possibilities that are going to require extra stamina and courage:

Relive past successes. Make a list, mental or on paper, of the times you've tried and succeeded. Here is a powerful mental image: Braid a rope of past achievements to hang on to, both in good times and challenging ones.

Release past disappointments. Make another list of disappointments, and then tear it up, literally or figuratively. Shred it, set fire to it, flush it, and toss it in the waste basket. Gone!

Rehearse future possibilities. Produce, direct, and star in a mental movie of yourself exploring this wonderful possibility. See yourself meeting the challenges, bouncing back from any setbacks, and continuing on with energy and determination.

When you go all-out pursuing potential possibilities, your attitude becomes more positive, your energy increases, and your courage strengthens. Even if things don't turn out exactly as you had hoped, you've permanently boosted your attitude and resilience, keeping yourself open to new possibilities in the future.

If you start with the belief that possibilities are abundant and within your grasp, you will begin to see all the new opportunities available to you. If your belief is negative, you will see barriers instead. We all want to feel our opinions are correct. Therefore, if your opinion is that you have the ability to achieve great things, great things appear. But if you are convinced you're mediocre, you will only notice the average. To further support this diminishing belief in yourself, you will actually *ignore* the extraordinary abilities you have and focus your attention solely on your average attributes! It's time to take on a "poohsitive" attitude and *think again!*

Accept the challenges so that you can
feel the exhilaration of victory.

— GEORGE S. PATTON

FEAR VERSUS ANXIETY

The famous actor Laurence Olivier was so afraid of driving that whenever his car approached a red light, he'd step on the gas. He reasoned that the sooner he passed through "danger," the better. It's amazing he survived to win four Oscars and eleven Oscar nominations.

Putting aside such an irrational response, fear is fundamentally a useful and practical emotion. It alerts us to potential dangers so we can take adequate precautions to avoid them. Fear is usually inspired by some real likelihood. Facts indicate we will face a bad outcome unless we keep our brakes fixed, child-proof our homes when we have little ones, change the batteries in our smoke detectors, and practice good health habits.

Fear can also be a good indicator that we are stretching, growing, and challenging ourselves. It keeps us alert and focused. Great possibilities are rarely realized through comfortable circumstances. Great possibilities require risks, and taking risks generates fear. Adequately addressed, such fear doesn't have to hold us back.

Anxiety, on the other hand, is an entirely useless emotion. It is a product of our imagination. Anxiety anticipates a negative event, even a remote or impossible one, with such intensity that we can be immobilized. Anxiety is a disabling roadblock to possibilities. It distorts our vision and disrupts momentum, distracting and discouraging us. When we are gripped by anxiety, we focus on everything that could possibly go wrong. There's no energy left to think about what can, might, or must go right.

Have you ever felt as if a huge boulder was on your chest? Have you felt weighed down by a sense of impending doom? This was most likely anxiety. Now, think about the last time you tried something new or different. How did you feel? Would you agree that every time you have achieved something extraordinary you were nervous or a bit scared? Going for a job interview, asking someone for a date, making a speech—most people experience a little bit of fear, but did you also feel anxiety? Was it a useful emotion?

The word *fear* comes from the Old English word *faer*, meaning sudden danger. Today, we see fear as an emotional reaction to real danger. Here is my own definition with a more positive view: "Fear is an emotional response to real possibilities."

Anxiety comes from the Latin word *anxius*, which means to be troubled in the mind by an uncertain event. Another definition is to press tightly or strangle. The key words are "troubled" and "mind." The provoking thought is neither identifiable nor reality based. Here is my own definition: "Anxiety is anything that suffocates your possibilities." Anxiety is an emotional barrier because it causes us to resist possibilities.

Fear heightens alertness, which can serve as a catalyst to propel us towards exciting new possibilities. Use it to your advantage to accomplish remarkable things!

If we all did the things we are capable of
doing, we would literally astound ourselves.

— THOMAS EDISON

THE "GO!" TECHNIQUE

There's a popular behavior-modification technique called "thought-interruption." The idea is that whenever a negative idea pops into your head, you shout, "Stop!" or imagine a big stop sign. This strategy is supposed to help people interrupt their worry/anxiety cycle before it gains momentum.

However, this system of thought-interruption violates one of the principles of possibility language, which is to use *positive* terms only. Saying "Stop" causes a negative reaction and is a bit like telling someone, "Don't think about elephants." They're going to think about elephants! I'd like to suggest a more positive "possibility" approach, one that my audiences have responded to with great enthusiasm.

Whenever you catch yourself indulging in unproductive anxieties, visualize a red light changing to a huge green one. Shout, "Go!" and step on the gas, leaving your anxious thoughts behind. Put yourself in the driver's seat and take the anxiety-free, "possibility" road.

Some people engage in a sort of backwards magical thinking: "If I vividly visualize failure, then it won't actually occur." It's like the tradition in some societies of demeaning everything precious so the gods won't be jealous and take the good things away. ("Oh, *this* old thing!") But here's the news. Anticipating a negative outcome from our efforts does *not* prevent bad things from happening. It may actually help to bring them about. It's like "rehearsing" doom, creating a self-fulfilling prophesy.

But what about doing this instead? Rather than visualizing disaster, dedicate all that effort and energy to believing your intentions are possible. Your chances for achieving them are much greater.

If you're still not convinced, analyze your anxiety-producing thoughts. How are they beneficial? What are the payoffs? How uncomfortable would you be if you decided to dump them? If you're like me, this exercise will show that anxiety produces only new problems, not new possibilities.

In my book *How High Can You Bounce?* I explain how "motion affects emotion." When you're feeling stalled or stymied, the best way to jump-start yourself is literally to get moving. Working your muscles, getting your blood pumping, and inhaling oxygen all stimulate your brain to produce the chemicals it needs to function happily and efficiently.

Interestingly, "emotion affects motion" is also true. Motion—your energy level and stamina—is profoundly influenced by emotions. When you are inspired by possibilities, your body and brain get a continuous jolt of chemical signals that keep them functioning at peak level. Athletes describe this as being "in the zone." Just the thought of what you might be able to achieve propels you out of bed, eager for whatever's ahead. The boring, tedious things we all face daily, even stress, become insignificant because you see the big picture. When your possibilities are compelling, and attitude positive, most of your hours are lived with zest, enthusiasm, and joy. You notice options and openings, that you would have been blind to, because you're *looking* for them. Ready, set…

CLEAN YOUR CLOSETS

Have you ever had a closet full of nothing to wear? That was my dilemma. I wear an odd size. Because I have very short arms and legs, I am not an off-the-rack kind of guy. Let's put it this way... the only one who wears the same size as me is a dachshund!

This has been a continual challenge, especially with my hectic travel schedule. In my profession I have to be presentable, so my solution was to buy anything that sort of fit and make do. If something actually fit, I'd wear it until it fell to pieces. If nothing fit, I'd go out and buy something new. Eventually, the closets were bursting. Yet, the more clothes I had, the harder it was to get dressed.

One day, my wife Kathryn had had enough. She insisted I get rid of everything worn-out, outdated, or that didn't fit. Furthermore, following this radical purge, I could not go right out and buy more clothes. "You'll find you have everything you need and more," she assured me.

Very reluctantly, I began to sort, and it was just amazing. Clothes kept appearing, like clowns from one of those clown cars, and I kept saying, "Now, where did *that* come from?" And an astonishing thing happened. After the Big Clear-Out, it was as if I had a whole new wardrobe of clothes I couldn't remember buying. Kathryn was right (as always). My clothing struggle of finding something acceptable to wear was

THINK AGAIN

over, until I wore out all the "new" clothes I had rediscovered. Only then was I found at the store.

When you get rid of the useless stuff, you often discover that you already have most or all of what you really need. Here's how that applies to possibilities. As you analyze your past and present, think about what you can let go of so you can find something new. Do you have beliefs that are worn or outdated? Perhaps you are clothing yourself in actions and attitudes that no longer fit. Have you outgrown low expectations of yourself?

Here are some outmoded thinking habits you may not need anymore:

"I've been dealt a bad hand, so why bother?"

"I tried, but I don't have what it takes."

"People like me can only dream about that."

"Other people get all the breaks."

Dump obsolete beliefs. Here are new thinking habits to help generate possibilities:

"I'm starting with a new deck."

"I've learned a lot for my next try."

"Dreaming is just the beginning."

"My unique perspectives give me the edge."

84

Maybe it's time to get rid of old thinking that may be obscuring your possibilities and limiting your potential. Time to *think again*, clothed in a new wardrobe.

You don't have to have more or be more before anything can happen.

THE LANGUAGE OF POSSIBILITIES

One of the most possibility-limiting words in the English language is "improbable." It is like a big, black wall, effectively blocking any further effort or consideration. While some may say it can't be done because of the obstacles, peak performers move towards their goals regardless of the barriers. When faced with inevitable obstacles, possibility-seekers use a different vocabulary – a "language of possibilities" – to describe options and opportunities." If someone says, "That's really not likely" or "This would be much safer," the minds of possibility-seekers *think again*. "*Why* isn't it likely?" "What would happen if...?" "Could I try it *this* way instead?" They develop a unique questioning style, a powerful tool for expanding possibilities.

Extreme language portrays things as black and white with no tantalizing in-between. It can discourage possibility thinking with either/or words like "never" and "always," "must" and "mustn't," "mandatory" and "forbidden." Here are a few examples.

NON-POSSIBILITY LANGUAGE	POSSIBILITY LANGUAGE
Never	Maybe – could be
Always	Sometimes
Forever	Temporarily
Absolutely	Perhaps

Forbidden	Reconsidered
Compulsory	Optional
Discouraged	Encouraged
Behave	Struggle
Suitable	Imaginative
Normal	Exceptional
Acceptance	Exploration
Respectful	Questioning
Respectable	Provocative
Staid	Inspirational
Customary	Creative
Traditional	Innovative
Disaster	Opportunity
Success	Opportunity
An end	A beginning
Destiny, fate	Common sense, curiosity
That's just how it is.	Why?
No one's ever done that.	Why not?

Language is the power tool of possibilities. It's not just the words we use, but how we *frame* ideas so they inspire us to see possibilities in new ways.

There's the classic story of the time Steve Jobs was trying to talk John Sculley, a top executive at Pepsi-Cola, into becoming the CEO of Apple Computer. Jobs flew from Silicon Valley in California to New York and sat in Sculley's Manhattan office with its breathtaking view. Sculley was not enthusiastic. He had a list of demands that included a huge salary, huge bonus, and a huge severance package. Not only that, he wouldn't leave New York. He'd be a consultant for Apple from his New York office.

How did Steve Jobs convince John Sculley to take the position and to move from New York City to California? He helped him *think again* and see the extraordinary possibilities with a simple word picture: *"Do you want to sell sugar water for the rest of your life, or do you want to change the world?"*

Dwell in possibility.

— EMILY DICKINSON
POET

BLUE GENES

Psychologists have a saying: "We have *traits* (inborn) and we have *states* (chosen)." Depression can be both. The negative feelings, physical and emotional, that arise from depression and negativity are champion opportunity blockers. For example, when choosing what socks to wear is overwhelming, making positive decisions about significant life choices is impossible. Fortunately, medical science is making huge advances in treating debilitating disorders. And one of the best re-discoveries made is that our thoughts have a tremendous impact on our feelings.

People aren't optimistic *because* they have recognized possibilities. They recognize possibilities *because* they are *optimistic*. Maybe you've heard someone say, "I was born pessimistic. That's how my brain works." The implication is that they were born to think negatively. They are convinced it's genetically programmed into their DNA. "I came into this world with curly hair, brown eyes, and a negative attitude." If this is your belief, *think again*. A negative mind-set is definitely a big barrier to seeing new possibilities.

Just like everyone else, I was born with some unchangeable physical characteristics. And just like everyone, at times I struggle to remain positive and accept what I can't change. However, a major turning point in my life took place when I discovered I had the power to be a "super hero." No, I couldn't leap tall buildings with a single bound, and the only bird I was ever mistaken for was a stork! But I do have X-ray vision; I can see through the brick walls of negativity that well-meaning people build in my path. You can have that same powerful vision.

Being born with an unchangeable physical challenge forced me to look *within* for something that *was* changeable, for something I *could* control. Suddenly, I realized what it was! The greatest obstacle to my success was not my hands or legs. It was how I *viewed* them. Real power happens when we take complete control over our *perspective*.

When you take control over the attitudes and beliefs that are holding you back, you accept responsibility for your choices. You choose whether to notice and evaluate possibilities. You can choose which opportunities to jump at and which to reject because they are not in line with your values and goals. You become an active driver, rather than passive passenger, of your life.

When I was a kid, busy making excuses to get out of things I didn't want to do, I'd play the "physically-challenged" card. I thought of it as my ace in the hole. Oh, was I good! What I never seemed to learn was that my father was playing a different game, and he held the trump card. He wanted me to succeed on the world's terms, and that didn't leave any room for "poor me-ism." He'd confront my negativity with a comment like, "Move out of pity city!" His admonition was he wanted me to look *inside* myself, to look at my state of mind, instead of in the mirror at my physical traits. Yes, the shape of my hands and legs, and my cranium pattern baldness (darn!), are predetermined genetic traits. My choice to become excited about possibilities and explore them is not.

I choose to *think again* and live in the powerful state of possibility. How about you?!

A POSSIBILITY IN A TRAFFIC JAM

It is a very humbling experience to have a career as a motivational speaker and to parent teenagers. I wish you could be a guest around our dinner table as we discuss family issues. If one of the kids is struggling with something, I've been known to launch into my best podium material, words that have inspired the applause of hundreds of thousands of people. "Challenges are inevitable," I'll proclaim in my most persuasive tones. "Defeat is optional." And three pairs of eyes give me blank looks followed by deep sighs and mutterings of, "Whatever."

Recently, I was in the car with my three teenagers. As we drove along, I was grumbling to myself about the near-gridlock traffic and how tremendously important it was that we not be late. I was leaning so close to the steering wheel that I considered taking a bite out of it to relieve my stress. My complaining escalated until one of my kids said, "Sounds like Dad needs to pull over and read his own book."

Oh, they had a hearty laugh, and I was reminded to ask myself, "Will the world come to an end if we're late?" The truth is that no real damage would be done. It would be an inconvenience but not important in the long run. I was wasting an excellent opportunity to chat with my kids and notice the scenery. I was overlooking an invaluable possibility: the chance to build our relationship, and maybe even create a moment that they – and I – might remember all our lives.

A note on roadblocks. As you pursue possibilities, you will invariably encounter traffic jams. It is inevitable. An important thinking strategy is to be *ready* for them. "Aha," you might be saying, "but that's contrary to what you said about not anticipating negative outcomes." It's vital, however, to *acknowledge* that you're going to run into roadblocks (and overcome them) as a basic principle of staying optimistic. You'll maintain a buoyant attitude because you are seldom surprised by setbacks. You accept that they are an inescapable reality of life.

The ability to hang in there in spite of obstacles is essential if we are to realize our possibilities. Whenever you hit a wall and feel like quitting, *think again*. Even the best planning and forethought will not prevent all unexpected obstacles. When you encounter roadblocks, your initial response may be to floor it—in reverse. But if you anticipate barriers, you can respond positively by slowing down and deciding whether the best course of action is to go around it, through it, or over it.

Choice, not chance, determines your possibilities.

FINDING A PARKING SPACE

I once knew a man named Dave Martin who boasted that he could always find a parking spot, no matter how difficult the situation. I watched him, and by golly, he invariably did! He confided that he'd paid a psychic to enhance this ability.

Had he actually acquired some supernatural or extrasensory power? Or was it that his belief in the possibility tuned him into signals that others would overlook? A man striding down the street with his hand in his pocket might be reaching for his car keys. A woman passing between parked cars while carrying packages might be about to the put them in a trunk and drive off. However, if Dave had convinced himself that his lot in life was to circle the block endlessly, he would have ignored any clues that a space was opening up.

It's the chicken-and-egg paradox. Which comes first? When you're aware of possibilities, you throw your mind, body, and soul into pursuing them. You work in your "zest zone," feeling invigorated instead of exhausted. Awareness helps you see a future filled with hope, confidence, and optimism—a future full of possibilities.

We all visualize the outcome of our efforts. The difference is that some people see what they *don't* want. Others have a vivid picture of what they want and see it happening. They believe it *can* happen. Visualization is a power tool for possibilities. When you project your mind forward and see a clear picture of your possibilities being realized, it's an amazing force that moves you toward them. Achieving possibilities begins with an "inside job" instead of external actions.

Using this technique of mental "rehearsal," you can make current possibilities into future achievements. Actors, speakers, and athletes rehearse what they plan to do until it comes automatically and effortlessly. You can do the same. Here are some guidelines for effective possibility-visualization.

Relax. Take a deep breath and begin to release any tension you may be experiencing. Breathe deeply until your body and mind are calm. Something I find helpful is to identify my doubts and, as I am exhaling, to visualize the doubts being blown away. I have witnessed many successful athletes use this relaxation exercise to reprogram their minds and prepare for victory.

Recall. Take a moment to identify a previously successful experience that clearly shows your competence and self-confidence. Resist recalling past hurts or disappointments so you can fortify your resolve. As you do this, start to affirm yourself by making sure your thoughts are positive, personal, and embrace possibilities.

Rehearse. Have you ever said, "I knew that would happen"? Most likely you were visualizing–either negatively or positively. Focus on the positive. Imagine you actually doing and saying exactly what is needed for success. Before important events, I visualize right before I go to sleep. I see a positive outcome and then I "sleep on it." It is amazing how much better you sleep when you look forward to the next day with excitement rather than dread.

Now go out and find those front-row parking spots that have your name on them.

TASTING THE HOT DOGS

It was a baseball fan's dream: to be in the stands on the historic day when Cal Ripken of the Baltimore Orioles would break Lou Gehrig's record for consecutive games played. The 1996 game was completely sold out, and dignitaries from all over the world were competing for seats. However, my friend Phil Hempfing was undaunted.

Phil had hired me to speak when he was a school superintendent in Hanover, Pennsylvania. He was an avid baseball fan, and attending this game was a dream come true! Phil was able to secure tickets through a friend, and at five o'clock he stood in line at will call. But when his turn came, the ticket agent said Phil's name wasn't on the list. You can imagine how he felt. A one-time event in the history of baseball, and his name wasn't on the list!

But Phil was determined to realize his possibilities... He politely suggested that the agent recheck her records. He waited as the rest of the people in line passed inside. The ticket agent returned and said she was sorry, but they had no record of a Phil Hempfing. It was now 6:20 PM, and the game would start at 7:00.

Many human reactions are possible at such a moment, some negative and unproductive. Phil chose the positive approach, pleading with her to search again. "I had visualized being there so strongly," Phil told me later, "that

I could even taste the hot dogs. I hadn't come this far to give up now."

Did Phil's perseverance pay off? As he was standing at the ticket counter, a representative from the Orioles overheard his conversation. He was clearly impressed with Phil's tenacity and, more importantly, his optimistic attitude. He handed Phil a ticket and said, "Enjoy the game." Phil told me he was overwhelmed with emotion as he took his seat, in the front row! Well, if you've ever seen the famous picture of Cal Ripken facing the Oriole dugout with the fans cheering wildly, then you've seen Phil Hempfing. He was seated near President Bill Clinton, Tom Hanks, and other world-renowned celebrities.

You see, sometimes possibilities often happen if you just hang in there and never give up. When someone asks me what is the first step to success, I simply say, "Show up and stay up!" In other words, make a decision to take action and remain possibility focused no matter what resistance you face. It may be your priceless ticket to success!

Let me tell you the secret that has led to my goal: My strength lies solely in my tenacity.

— LOUIS PASTEUR
CHEMIST KNOWN FOR HIS
LIFE-SAVING WORK

CHARIOTS AND TRUMPETS

When the ancient Romans wanted to make Julius Caesar a god, he ordered a servant to ride just behind him in the chariot during triumphal processions. The crowds cheered their heads off, trumpets blew, and beautiful women swooned as he was pelted with flower petals. Yet, through it all, the servant, on Caesar's order, kept repeating in his ear: "You are only a man. You are only a man..."

It's far too easy to get an exaggerated idea of our own importance. Sometimes I come home from an especially successful presentation. With applause and praise ringing in my ears, I turn into the driveway and wonder why a red carpet hasn't been rolled out for me. No trumpets, no rose petals. My wife and kids soon return my ego to normal size.

I always fall for this one! Someone will call and ask, "Hey Roger, do you believe in free speech?" My reply was, "Of course I believe in free speech." "Happy to hear that. How about giving a free one to my group?!"

I had placed on my calendar a freebie, speaking before an audience of 500 physically-challenged adults. By the way, I only speak to groups of disabled people. Isn't it true we all have "handicaps"? Some you can see, many you cannot. Soon after confirming the engagement, a corporate client (paying) called and requested the same day. I had a dilemma: should I call my free speech audience and cancel? The fact was, the month was lasting longer than my money, and I needed an extra date on the calendar! I thought, "Of course these people have an idea of who I am—a big-cheese corporate speaker. They will understand I am one important dude, and if they are not aware of this, all they have to do is ask me!" My self-aggrandizement became so intense I stood outside feeling I might burst and mess up my office!

Then, thankfully, I stopped and *thought again*. My career was built by speaking in front of audiences for no fee. I would temporarily increase my bank account but permanently damage my reputation and character.

I swallowed my dangerously inflated ego and went. They turned out to be one of the most memorable audiences I have ever had, teaching me more about possibilities than I was able to teach them. It was a humbling reality check and much-needed reminder of my early days in the speaking business. When I started out talking to school kids and other audiences, they didn't care how important I thought *I* was. They only cared how important I could make *them* feel. It was true then, and it's twice as true today.

On my way home I thought, "Okay Roger, you could be staying in a luxury resort being pampered and eating your favorite… swordfish." Did I really miss it? Nah. I went and had a fish sandwich at McDonalds.

Don't let ego and a lack of humility deprive you of possibilities. What does "humility" mean? And why should you care? You may wonder why I stop so often to analyze the origins of the words we use every day. It's because this background can provide unexpected insight and understanding. But I have to admit that before I wrote this book, I did not have the humility to explore the meaning of the word "humility." It is a nice word, a concept that is thought of favorably, but somewhat difficult to define. It's one of those "I know it when I see it" kind of words.

We'd be unlikely to make a connection between "humility" and "possibility," but, as I've learned more about the people and organizations who exemplify possibility thinking, the characteristics of humility have become evident. Humility is a positive value in all our lives, but it is even more than that. The practice of humility can lead us to even greater possibilities.

Let's look first at what humility is *not*. It means the quality of being humble, not arrogant. It comes from the same Latin root, but is not synonymous with "humiliated." Humility doesn't imply that you are powerless and pitiful. It does not have to include an attitude of meekness or victimhood.

There is a popular flippant statement that clearly shows a lack of humility: "Been there, done that." This implies that you've gotten all you need from an experience and have no need to learn more. However, one of the paradoxes of life is that the more you know, the more you realize how much you *don't* know. A truth I've learned from the examples in this book is that possibilities are realized by continuing to grow and expand my awareness, no matter what I have already learned or accomplished.

Humility, as I define it, is a sincere interest in others, knowing that everyone has something to teach us. It is also an open-minded approach to life that encourages the flexible thinking that sparks possibilities. Those lacking humility are so self-focused that they rarely have time to learn from others. Remember the old joke of the egocentric celebrity who says, "But enough about me. How do *you* feel about me?"

Yet, being humble does not eliminate self-assuredness or self-confidence. In fact, both are important characteristics of humble people.

One word you rarely associate with humility is "greed." However, humble people are usually greedy—voracious to learn from the viewpoints and wisdom of others. They possess a child-like fascination with the world around them. Far from being a contradiction, "ambition" is also an essential component of humility, making us eager to spot and pursue possibilities.

Humility is not only an attitude, but also a way of being. Do you remember the best selling book, *I'm OK, You're OK*, by Thomas A. Harris? I like to paraphrase that title: "I'm not always OK, nobody is always OK, and that's OK." The fact is, I am no better or no worse a person than anyone else. Accept, with humility and pride, the reality that you have your own unique resources, talents, and passions. Then *think again* with confidence about the unlimited possibilities available to the unique you.

There's nothing so becomes a man as
modest stillness and humility.

— WILLIAM SHAKESPEARE

THE PHANTOM GARAGE DOOR

Our neighbor was having trouble with his automatic garage-door opener. The door would open at unexpected times, both day and night. Sometimes he would come home to find it open and his dogs out relandscaping the neighbors' yards. Late at night, he would hear the gears grinding. He'd run downstairs to find the door open, but no one in sight.

First, he called the manufacturer. They told him that he had one of the first models on the market, the granddaddy of all openers, and that his remote signal could not be changed or reprogrammed. However, they agreed to check out his system. A repairman came and studied the door. It might be interference from a police scanner or radio station, the repairman decided. He also confirmed that the opener could not be reprogrammed and advised my neighbor to buy a newer model.

Being frugal and highly suspicious that this advice was just a sales pitch, my neighbor determined to find a solution short of buying a whole new mechanism. He spent several months looking for a pattern in the unexpected garage-door openings, but there were none.

Still, he absolutely refused to buy a new opener. (Did I mention he was frugal?) Finally, he disconnected the opening device. I would drive by and see him pulling into his driveway, stopping the car, and climbing out to yank on the handle and haul the door up with an angry grunt. After pulling in and shutting off the car, he would repeat the operation and, with a whoosh of air, the door would slam down and smack against the pavement. Rain or shine, he had to get out of his car and pull the door open. The process didn't seem to be doing much for his blood pressure or the door. He could have purchased a new garage-door opener, but he refused to do so on principle. After three years of raising and lowering the garage door by hand, he put his house up for sale and moved away.

The new owner wondered why the automatic garage-door opener wasn't working and quickly discovered it was unplugged. He located the remotes, reconnected the opener, and felt proud that he had solved the first problem with his new house. Except that within a week, the door creaked open while he was enjoying dinner. The next time it opened itself was late at night. He and his wife thought they were being robbed. The third time, he was retrieving his newspaper early in the morning and noticed the door eerily swing open. And no one was in sight up or down the street.

Again, our new neighbor sought out an expert, a "garage-door electronics specialist" from San Francisco. The specialist was standing in the driveway with my neighbor, diagnosing the problem, when I drove past the house after an early morning tennis match. My usual routine is to turn the corner onto my street and press my automatic door remote to open my garage. My house is second from the corner, and by the time I reach it, my garage door is open, and I pull right in. As usual, I depressed the button on my remote and then waved to my new neighbor. As I drove into my garage, I glanced in my rearview mirror and noticed the two men running toward my house. They raced up to me in the garage. "Hand over your clicker!" they shouted.

Their faces were flushed, they were panting, and I thought it best to obey and ask questions later. They grabbed the remote and raced back to my neighbor's front yard. I curiously followed them. The specialist held my remote in his right hand and extended his arm, pointing the remote at my neighbor's garage door. Click. The door rattled open.

Laughter echoed down the street, and my new neighbor's laughter was the loudest. He could barely catch his breath. Because of a jog in the road and the positions of our houses, I had never been able to see that my remote was also opening a second garage door down the street. And by the time my neighbor ran out, I would already be inside my garage with the door closed, striding into my kitchen.

Normally, one might be able to figure this out because of the schedule of the neighbor with the rogue remote. However, I keep no set schedule. I leave for the airport at all hours of the day, often returning in the middle of the night. Thus, there had never been any pattern to the ghostly openings.

My neighbor and I were both happy that the mystery had been solved. Riddled with undeserved guilt and kicking myself that I had never made the possible connection, I reprogrammed my remote (easy to do with my model) and ended the problem.

This incident made me realize how often we overlook what is right under our noses and look outside our own capabilities, hoping that an "expert" can solve our problems and point us in the right direction. Often we *do* need outside help, but sometimes the real expertise is as close as Dorothy's ruby slippers were to her getting home on her own. We often have the potential and expertise within ourselves, if we just *think again* and ask the right questions.

The problems of the world cannot possibly be solved by skeptics or cynics whose horizons are limited by the obvious realities. We need men who can dream of things that never were.

— PRESIDENT JOHN F. KENNEDY

3

AMPLIFY YOUR POTENTIAL

What are your assets?

THE PARABLE OF THE TALENTS

In ancient times, a talent was a weight, sometimes used to measure silver. It came to signify a monetary unit or something of great value. The *Bible* offers the Parable of the Talents in Matthew 25:15-40, using the silver variety of talent as a metaphor. It explains the behavior needed to achieve heaven, but it is easy to apply the parable's message to the more intangible kind of talents we possess and how we use them here on earth.

The story starts, "For the kingdom of heaven is as a man traveling into a far country, who called his own servants, and delivered unto them his goods." This traveler entrusts his fortune to his three servants to guard while he is gone. To the first servant he gives five talents (a lot of money); to the second, he gives two; and to the third, the one he trusts least, he gives only one talent. The first two risk the money by investing it. Fortunately, they are successful and able to hand their master double on his return, which makes him very happy: "Well done, good and faithful servant," he tells both of them.

The third servant is so concerned about not losing his master's money that he buries his coin. Thus, when the master returns, the money is safe, but there is still only the single talent. Is the master content? Hardly. He cries, "Thou wicked and slothful servant" and throws the man out. The message is that it's wrong to have talents and not use them. We must invest and multiply them.

An important point of the parable is that everyone is given talents in different amounts. What really matters is not what talents we have, but what we *do* with them. What if the servant with five talents had risked and lost them all? Would the master have been as happy? Would he have forgiven him? We'll never know for sure. What if the first two servants had lost everything, and the master returned to find that his entire remaining wealth consisted only of the single buried talent? Then servant number three would have been the *hero* of the story. Once again, we'll never know for sure. Parables are stories designed to teach, so the intended message is we must *risk* using our talents, win or lose.

No doubt you can think of a few individuals who have experienced great success in life with just a single talent, sometimes even a modest one. They combined this talent with their resources and passions to achieve great things. They took a risk and made it possible.

You, I, and nearly everyone else have a variety of talents—useful ones, important ones, even silly ones like being able to wiggle your ears. Composer Noël Coward wrote a poignant lyric about a singer who laments, "The most I've had is just a talent to amuse." But even so, singing is a wonderful talent and one that makes the world much richer. In fact, Coward chose the phrase as the title for one of his autobiographies. He recognized the importance in his own life of using one's talents.

EXERCISE:

Get out a piece of paper and write a list of the things you are really good at. As you expand your possibility thinking, you may find yourself covering both sides of the sheet; keep going. If it helps, start with the big categories: marketing, managing, designing, abstract thinking, leadership, etc. But don't stop there and don't disparage your talents if you're not at the top of your field. Keep going. Your potential is still there, waiting for you to make connections.

Do you make a great pot of chili? Are you skilled at parallel parking? Balancing your checkbook? Keeping a hula-hoop going? Remembering names? Planning a trip? Making people feel good in stressful situations? Growing things? Fixing things? Recognizing bird calls? What separate skills and natural abilities—what *talents*—go into these activities? How can you combine and connect them to achieve your goals and your ideal life?

When I stand before God at the end of my life, I would hope that I would not have a single bit of talent left, and could say, "I used everything you gave me."

— ERMA BOMBECK

WHAT ARE YOU REALLY BAD AT?

What are you gifted at? The popular wisdom is that we must struggle to improve the areas in which we are weakest—that we should always be pushing our boundaries, no pain-no gain, etc. *Think again!*

Instead, figure out what you are really good at and then go for it! Figure out what you are *really* bad at—separating *real* from *imaginary*—and then figure a way around it. Either eliminate that skill from your job/life description or, more positively, find skilled people or professional services that will fill in the gap and take up the slack. You don't have to do everything perfectly.

Everyone has talents. We choose how we see them, and we choose how we use them. Does great training help to build on those talents and achieve possibilities? Without a doubt. Training is a valuable ingredient in achievement, influencing *what* we can become, but not *who* we can become. In fact, exceptional talent plus exceptional training does not *guarantee* exceptional possibilities. You still need to do exceptional thinking.

Are some people born hardwired to achieve greatness? Well, of course. There are the prodigies of the world, and then there are the rest of us. Fortunately, the rest of us have almost limitless possibilities to choose from. However, some individuals have decided they have been preprogrammed to fail. They wear the label "Born Loser" like a badge of honor. They figure their lot in life has been predetermined, so why fight it?

Here is a great philosophy for possibility living. Your potential will rise to the level of your expectations. I have often wondered how successful underachievers could be if they worked as hard on their expectations as they do on their excuses. Far too often, audience members will approach me after one of my presentations and tell me all the reasons they have for not realizing their possibilities. Many times, their stories are so creative that, if they put their words to music, they'd have a hit country-western song.

My hope is that, after they get home, they'll *think again* about their potential and come up with new possibility-oriented lyrics. In other words, that they'll play their current song backwards. There's an old joke that goes, "What do you get when you play a country-western recording backwards? You get your wife back, you get your truck back, and you get your dog back."

What lies behind us and what lies before us
are small matters to what lies within us.

— RALPH WALDO EMERSON
AMERICAN ESSAYIST AND POET

IT'S CURTAINS

For weeks, my daughter Monica had been rehearsing for the big holiday concert. It was to be a gala evening with several different youth choirs and orchestras performing. The big night finally came, and the audience was full of proud parents. First, there was the junior choir performance, followed by a violin and piano duet, and then an orchestral recital and another choral performance.

Between each segment, the huge velvet curtain glided shut and an announcer would introduce the next group. Monica's turn came at last, and her choir sang beautifully. As any impartial parents would, of course, Kathryn and I were just sure we could hear Monica's voice clearly among all the other voices. The curtain closed, the choir exited the stage, and the next group, a concert band, took their place behind the closed curtain. Their musical selections were introduced, and the audience applauded expectantly.

But the curtain didn't open. It was stuck. Hurried whispers, some rushing about back stage, murmuring parents, and a rustling of young feet behind the thick velvet. A long pause. Still nothing.

Finally, Mrs. Leighton, my daughter's choir teacher, announced that the technician had been sent for, but could not arrive for at least twenty minutes. Making the best of the situation, she called for volunteers to help by holding the curtain up as far as possible, so the concert could continue. Willing parents and tuxedo-clad choir members trooped up on stage and hoisted the heavy velvet, groaning under its weight. Finally, an arched opening was made. We could see *all* of the band members in the exact center of the stage; then the headless bodies of those immediately left and right of center; then just the waists and legs of those further out; then their neighbors from the knees down; and finally, only the shoes of those near the ends of the rows. The unlucky lads and lasses on the extreme outer edges of the rows were invisible. At a signal from the director, the gallant band began to play, its sound slightly muffled by the velvet, as we gazed mostly at their uniformed legs and feet.

Finally, a shout went up backstage. A helpful parent had quietly located a tall ladder, scaled the behind-the-scenes equipment, and somehow figured out how to get the curtain machinery moving again. There was some clanking, the curtain shuddered, and then it slowly separated to reveal the full band, flushed and triumphant.

All the parents agreed that the kids looked fabulous and performed beautifully that evening, but the stars—the ones who got the loudest applause of the night—were Mrs. Leighton and the parents and students who had so gallantly improvised a way for the concert to continue.

Since I am a big fan of felines, I have reworded a popular statement. "There is more than one way to skin someone who does not like cats!"

There is more than one path towards possibilities. The key is to find your own path and keep an eye out for detours. We all have an opportunity to march to the beat of a different drummer. Do you hear possibility playing your song?

THE DEVIL MADE ME SAY IT

Have you ever heard the saying "Talk is cheap"? Think again about that statement. Talk can be very costly.

One afternoon, my wife and I were visiting with a mutual friend when he gave her a wonderful compliment. "Kathryn," he said, "you are like Ruth from the Bible–steadfast, kind, faithful, and loving." I smiled with appreciation, thinking how I had "out-married" myself. My facial expression must have communicated that I hoped he would identify some Biblical figure that I emulated. He got the hint.

"And Roger, *you* are like Boaz: strong, kind, and committed–a man of character."

After we parted, I reminisced about our conversation. I felt so blessed to have a wife like Ruth. Also, *I* was like… what was his name? All I remembered was that it started with a "B."

Several weeks later, Kathryn and I attended a party where we knew only a few people. The topic of conversation turned to the best qualities of our spouses. When my turn came, I said that my wife reminded me of Ruth in the Bible. I explained that a friend had pointed this out to me, and I agreed wholeheartedly. "And did he say anything about you?" someone asked. I smiled modestly; a little embarrassed to admit that my friend had also compared me to a well-respected Biblical figure.

"He said I was like... uhhh..." and I frantically tried to recall the "B" name "...*Beelzebub!*"

My wife blushed and was clearly overwhelmed. Well, when you're married to a person whose character is like that of a Biblical figure, it *is* a bit awe-inspiring.

"Roger," she said quietly, "I don't think you mean that."

"I certainly *do*," I replied confidently. Then I looked around the room. I had not seen expressions like that since the time I told 1,000 people at a national sales meeting to "Enjoy great success this year," but it had come out as "Enjoy great sex this year."

By now, Kathryn was desperate to save me from myself and salvage our reputations. "He means '*Boaz,*'" she hastily announced to the group, a few of whom looked unconvinced. Then, in a fierce whisper to me, she said: "Roger, Beelzebub is the *devil!*"

My wife and I have known each other since we were twelve years old. This shared history is precious to us, filled with wonderful memories. That day we added another memory, one that I will never forget—nor live down. I'm also unlikely to forget the names of Boaz and Beelzebub ever again.

I'll also never forget the saying "The devil is in the details" meaning the details can cause failure. However, when it comes to possibilities, I believe the devil is in the *delay!* Failure to *think again* can lead to procrastination, and we miss an opportunity to succeed. Instead, we need to zip the lip, run like the devil, and race towards possibilities.

THE FUTURE FARMERS
TEACH ME ENGLISH

Kids have a keen "baloney detector." If you ever want to reduce an inflated ego or get a firm reality-check, try talking to
them. They'll tune out at the slightest hint of disingenuous-
ness or lack of authenticity.

During the past twenty-five years, I've been privileged
to speak before hundreds of high school audiences. It's amazing how your exaggerated self-importance shrinks when you
watch them plug in their iPods and listen to their favorite
music as you are introduced. Standing before more than a
thousand kids in a stuffy gym, with a poor sound system,
during the last period of the day, on Friday afternoon, and
getting their attention—now, that's really good speaking!

So, there I was, addressing the California Future Farmers of America at the Fresno Convention Center and looking
into the faces of 4,000 of the liveliest teenagers I had ever
seen. The energy in that crowd reminded me of grade school
the day after Halloween, when everyone is on a sugar high.

I loved the enthusiasm of this audience! I matched their
energy with mine, and I *hope* they related to my life—maybe
not the actual experiences, but the *feelings* we've all had about
our experiences. I *willed* those iPods back in their pockets
as I made them laugh and, hopefully, *think again*. There
were 8,000 eyes following my every move, and when I was
through, their applause made the podium vibrate.

After my talk, a young man came on stage and presented me with an FFA sweatshirt. "Mr. Crawford showed us some mad skills today," he told the audience. The students erupted into applause as I smiled and acknowledged the gift. I remember thinking, "*Mad?* Does he mean 'angry' or 'mentally unstable'?" I hoped I hadn't communicated either.

As we walked backstage, I thanked the chairperson and my student hosts for the honor of being part of their conference. Then I risked asking, "What is a 'mad skill'?"

The kids chuckled at my terminal adultness. One explained, "It's what you're good at! Like if you're a good dancer, singer, mathematician, or athlete—it's your 'mad skill.' Mr. Crawford, you *kill* (impress) as a speaker, and you are *down with* (good at) tennis. You've got *mad* skills!"

I may not have spoken the language of these kids, but hopefully I had come across as someone they could relate to—a real person with struggles who could teach them something. And I learned from them that if you build your *downness*, you'll *kill* yourself with your own *mad* possibilities. Your potential is determined by discovering your "mad skills."

Language is the dress of thought.

— SAMUEL JOHNSON
CONSIDERED THE FINEST CRITIC
OF ENGLISH LITERATURE

EAGLES AND SLOTHS

I have no doubt you've had conversations like this. Our family was enjoying dinner together one night, and the question was posed, "What animal are you most like? What characteristics do you possess that suggest this animal?" We decided that we'd each state our choice, and then the others would debate how on-target we were.

The kids were intrigued and enthusiastically volunteered their wild kingdom identities. Christopher told us that he would be a bat. When he saw our puzzlement, he explained that bats are stealthy, agile, and have unseen abilities like supersonic hearing. Monica preferred a cat because they are graceful and you must earn their respect. Alexa's choice was a giraffe because she is tall and likes looking over the crowd.

Then it was my turn. Without hesitation, I blurted out that I was a sloth.

"A what?" everyone exclaimed.

"A three-toed sloth," I said. They looked bewildered.

I explained that since my foot was narrow and had only three toes, it resembled the foot of a sloth with its three claws. When I was a child, we had been studying pictures of animals in school. The teacher showed a photo of a sloth, and some of the kids started saying that I had a sloth foot. The less-than-flattering nickname stuck: "Super Sloth."

"Roger," my somewhat biased wife objected, "I disagree. Your physical challenge reminds *me* of an animal that you often emulate – an *eagle!* An eagle has three talons. You're strong and determined, and when you grab hold of something, you never let go."

It must be obvious by now that I firmly believe the greatest results can come out of working around a deficiency. Always remember that Michelangelo carved his masterpiece "David" from a block of marble that no other sculptor wanted. Even with all your weaknesses and defects, you still have the potential to be a masterpiece yourself.

EXERCISE:

Make a list of things that you believe are unique about you – useful things, admirable things, and irrelevant and silly things. Use your possibility thinking to fill a sheet of paper; keep going. Are you beginning to see how unique you are? No one else on earth has the same combination of abilities and experiences.

What talents do you already possess that make you great? What kinds of possibilities are within your reach now, and how can you obtain them? No one can do everything superbly, but all of us can do some things better than anyone else. What is *your* combination of abilities, limitations, enthusiasms, accomplishments, experiences, and aspirations that makes you unique? The truth is there has never been anyone exactly like you, and there never will be again. Even if you have an identical twin, just the things you've done and thought give you a unique take on the world around you.

Yes, you are an exciting tangle of incredible strengths and weaknesses, brilliance and blind spots. Opportunities open up when you leverage these wildly different components into a powerful whole. What tapestry of possibilities will your life create?

OUR DEEPEST FEAR

"Our deepest fear is not that we are inadequate. Our deepest fear is that we are powerful beyond measure. It is our light, not our darkness that most frightens us. We ask ourselves, Who am I to be brilliant, gorgeous, talented, fabulous? Actually, who are you not to be? You are a child of God. Your playing small does not serve the world. There is nothing enlightened about shrinking so that other people won't feel insecure around you. We are all meant to shine, as children do. We were born to make manifest the glory of God that is within us. It's not just in some of us; it's in everyone. And as we let our own light shine, we unconsciously give other people permission to do the same. As we are liberated from our own fear, our presence automatically liberates others."

— MARIANNE WILLIAMSON
AUTHOR

SISTERS CUTTING THE MUSTARD

Here I was in Portland, Oregon, seated at a banquet table prior to my speech. As the wait staff served the salads, I noticed something unusual. Instead of using the provided dressing, the audience members were opening jars sitting on their tables and slathering a yellow sauce over their greens. They also were putting a dollop on their plate and dipping their bread in it. As I watched my table mates ooh and ah over this obvious delight, I had to ask my seatmate what it was.

"Monastery Mustard," he replied. "It's the best in the world." He suggested I speak with Sister Terrie who had provided the samples for the group. As I approached her, she extended her arms in an enthusiastic embrace and said, "I am praying for you."

Taking this as a blessing rather than a warning, I asked her to tell me about Monastery Mustard. Her face lit up as she told me the history. Ten years earlier, the Benedictine Sisters of Mt. Angel had been facing two challenges. For eight decades, the Sisters had operated Mt. Angel Academy, Mt. Angel College, and other schools in the Willamette Valley. They also founded the nationally recognized Benedictine Nursing Center.

But now their retirement fund was not sufficient to support the more than 40 sisters in the Queen of Angels Monastery. In addition, they ran St. Joseph's Shelter which provided housing for homeless families and individuals. They discussed the traditional ways to raise money, the raffle ticket and bake-sale avenue, but they wanted to find something different and more effective. "Let's *think again*," they said.

One of their lay volunteers said, "I have this amazing mustard recipe passed down through my family. You could make it and sell it" The sisters thought it over and decided this had possibilities. They gathered the ingredients, experimented, and decided to give it a try. Between 4:00 and 5:30 AM each morning, a dozen sisters would prepare the day's supply, finishing just in time for morning prayers. At midmorning, another team of nuns would package the mustard in glass jars. The final inspection was done by the Mother Superior who blessed each jar as she sealed it.

The nuns began distributing their delicious mustard at farmers' markets throughout the Portland area. It was there that they met the Three Amigos, three teenaged boys who roasted Jalapeño peppers and sold them at the markets. The nuns noticed that customers were buying both products, dipping the peppers in the mustard. The sisters tried blending the peppers into their mustard, and, hallelujah – Hallelujah Jalapeño Mustard was born.

Other new flavors followed. The mustard is now offered in seven flavors including Glorious Garlic, Angelic Honey Garlic, Heavenly Honey, Devoutly Dill, Jubilant Blueberry, and Divinely Original. Their label shows a 1912 picture of the Monastery and a sister in the habit of their order. Because none of the actual sisters are depicted, they have named her Sister Generica.

Word began to spread beyond Oregon, and soon Monastery Mustard developed a national following. Specialty food stores started placing orders, and business boomed. A devoted fan nominated the mustard for the Mustard Hall of Fame. Monastery Mustard was inducted in 2003. Today, Monastery Mustard is distributed worldwide. But it is still made the same way, right before morning prayers, and is still sealed with a blessing.

I left the meeting hoping that I would see Sister Terrie again and that my wife could get the mustard stain out of my tie!

I tell you the truth, if you have faith as small as
a mustard seed, you can say to this mountain,
"Move from here to there" and it will move.

— JESUS CHRIST

WHAT'S BEHIND A NAME?

In 2006, Gary Johnson needed a new name for the business systems company he had just bought. He'd worked for this company as a salesman since 1990 and now wanted the name to reflect the new direction he planned to take. He had a dynamic organization that was experiencing tremendous growth in the copying, printing, and imaging business. He came up with a doozy.

"How did you come up with such a great name," I asked, "when the names of your competitors lack your creativity and are easily forgotten?" I assumed he'd say what I've heard numerous times: "Our advertising company chose it."

Instead, Gary said, "I was looking for something relevant to our industry, something that would be remembered for its uniqueness. One day I was walking around my office, thinking, when I focused on one of our products, a copy machine. When I saw the button labeled 'Zoom,' I had it!"

That's how Zoom Imaging Solutions got its name.

Nike, Rolex, and Starbucks are company names you recognize. Like Zoom Imaging Solutions, they were not named after a person. Disney, Ford, and Hewlett Packard are companies that carry the founder's name. Mental images appear when you think of these recognized companies.

Here's a question that is sure to conger up some interesting mental images. What would be the possibilities if you combined the rugged sport of football with women's under-garments? Could you "slip" by your defender? Have spaghetti strap shoulder pads? Wear a jersey that looked like a bustier? (And would former New York Jets quarterback, Joe Namath model it on TV?) But before you start making plans to watch the Chicago "Bares" in the Lingerie Bowl, *think again!*

Bennie Russell was an Alabama University football player in 1926. Practice after practice in the sweltering heat of the South, he and his teammates would sweat and chafe profusely while they wore the regulation wool jerseys. To say the least, this was an uncomfortable problem to have, but Bennie saw possibilities.

His father, Ben, owned Russell Manufacturing located in the small Alabama town of Alexander City. Their core business was manufacturing ladies undergarments. Benny watched his father making women's long johns and he saw a possibility. What if his dad made the teams' jerseys out of the thick, absorbent cotton used in the long johns? It would be cooler, more comfortable, and of course lighter weight.

Since the purpose of this product revolved around sweat, a mill worker came up with a name that has become an American icon...the sweatshirt. The company who originated the sweatshirt is now called Russell Athletic. So the next time you're relaxing in your favorite sweatshirt, thank a possibility thinker named Bennie Russell. The Einstein of sweat!

So many people say, "Oh, I could never be creative like that. If only I were smarter, better, more competent..." As kids, they came up with a hundred new ideas and solutions every hour, but somehow they lost touch with that inquiring, imaginative spirit. That spirit is your creativity. Bring it out of hiding.

Think like a child. Literally get down on all fours or up on a chair to consider a spatial problem. Turn things upside down and inside out, mentally and physically, to expand options. Imagine things happening backwards. Be silly if need be. It's amazing the solutions you can come up with.

Think "outside the box." This expression grew out of a connect-the-dots problem that can be solved only by extending the joining lines outside the grid of dots. Reconsider the "rules." Are they limiting your possible options? Can you rewrite them? Reverse them? Get around them?

Think again. What is the actual problem? Negotiators often find that people in conflict spend their time disagreeing about the specific route to their goal, when, in fact, a very different route to the same goal is available and mutually agreeable. Clarify the results you want, and then try redefining the steps necessary to achieve them.

What was the founder of a company thinking about when she started her business making chocolate-covered strawberries? Probably about customers like me who love chocolate and love strawberries.

I'll never forget the day refreshments were served prior to one of my speeches, and someone handed me a chocolate-covered strawberry that I eagerly accepted. It was challenging for me to hang on to the little green stem, and, as I bit into it, the berry exploded and dropped onto my shirt. Splat! The

135

stain looked as if I had been shot on the way to the podium. But there was no time to clean up or change. I was on.

My opening line of explanation was, "I got hit by a drive-by berry." It got a good laugh and motivated an audience member to introduce me to Shari Fitzpatrick, founder of Shari's Berries, maker of the irresistible confections.

Shari also loves chocolate and berries. When she was a banker, she used to make up homemade gift baskets of her dipped berries for her mortgage business customers. Her tactic worked. People remembered her, and they remembered her berry baskets.

Shari thought, "Wouldn't it be wonderful if I could market my gift baskets?" But, of course, people told her it would be impossible. Berries are seasonal and perishable, even covered in gourmet chocolate. Shari loves problem-solving almost as much as cooking. With a chorus of people telling her it was impossible, she did her homework and devised a way.

Shari opened her first store in Sacramento, California in 1989. She soon acquired three more nearby locations. Then she worked with packaging engineers to develop a foolproof method of shipping. When we met in 2005, Shari's Berries was dipping two million berries in more than sixty tons of toppings a year and shipping them throughout the world.

"How did you do it?" I had to ask.

Her smiling response was, "Just see possibilities before they become obvious to everyone else."

That's one of the powers of passion. Your passions open you to options and opportunities that no one else has spotted, yet.

We can't solve problems by using the same kind
of thinking we used when we created them.

> — ALBERT EINSTEIN
> PHYSICIST

ASK, CONNECT, PERSIST

There are three basic techniques that amplify our potential:

- Asking questions no one else has asked

- Making connections no one else has made

- Overcoming "impossible" obstacles

Asking questions no one else has asked: The right
question can be more important than the
right answer because it opens up all kinds of
possibilities. Helen Keller's teacher, Anne Sullivan,
changed the life of her blind and deaf student
by changing the question. Others were asking,
"What can we do with Helen?" Sullivan asked,
"What can I do *for* Helen?" Sullivan's answer was
to introduce the child to language, first by spelling
words into her hand and then through reading
Braille. Helen Keller went on to speak, graduate
with honors from Radcliffe College, master several
languages besides English, and write eloquent
books and articles. Her many friends included
kings, presidents, and Mark Twain. She changed
forever the public image of physically-challenged

people. Yet, she might have remained mute and uneducated if Anne hadn't asked the right question.

Making connections: In the 1988 film *Working Girl*, Melanie Griffith plays a secretary who puts together a multimillion dollar deal in her boss's absence. The boss returns and claims credit for the innovative concept. However, Griffith ultimately triumphs, demonstrating how she came up with the idea by melding a society page item with a clipping from the business section and a knowledge of current trade law. And, to clinch her claim to connection-making possibility thinking, she saves the huge merger from disaster at the last minute by pointing out a gossip column item in the morning paper. Historian James Burke has produced several lively PBS TV series about people who have connected apparently unrelated ideas to come up with world-changing devices and strategies—most of the wonders of the modern world. His title? *Connections.*

Overcoming "impossible" obstacles: In 1997, David Baldacci was just like thousands of other rather anonymous Washington, D.C. lawyers. Then, overnight, he became a best-selling author. His book *Absolute Power* got the highest advance ever for a first novel, and within days he had sold the movie rights for $1 million. The next year, *People* magazine proclaimed Baldacci one of the fifty sexiest people in the world.

David wrote his novel while working full-time as an associate at a Washington law firm and with a new baby at home. Few knew about his spare-time activity. But this *wasn't* his first novel. He had had numerous almost-deals in the past. His "instant" success took years of rejections and tantalizing near-breakthroughs. He knew people, had connections, but couldn't quite get things sold. He must have had close friends telling him, "Concentrate on your legal career" – "What about your new baby and family?" – "You've come so close over and over, it's obvious this isn't going to work!"

At a book signing, he told me that being a writer is like a "war of attrition" – a constant battle against the slow abrasion of discouragement and the exhausting demands of everyday life. "There are hundreds of other people who have the potential and could do the same thing, but most of them just can't keep slogging at it after work, day after day, and they drop out." Baldacci didn't. He did the impossible by never giving in to discouragement or the demands of life.

Never give in. Never give in. Never, never, never, never – in nothing, great or small, large or petty--never give in, except to convictions of honor and good sense.

— WINSTON CHURCHILL
PRIME MINISTER OF BRITAIN

SIX DEGREES OF SEPARATION

"It's not what you know, it's *who* you know" – and what *they* know. With about five billion people on the planet, that's a lot of possibilities. Someone came up with the idea of "six degrees of separation," suggesting that everyone on earth can now connect with any other specific individual in a meaningful way through a maximum of up to six varied relationships. For example, your brother has a French client, who went to school with a Brazilian, whose uncle is an archeologist, who knows the inhabitants of a remote Mongolian village. Thus, you have a way to secure an introduction to someone in that village and obtain some information or support you may want. Actually, I think six is an exaggeration. Often, such a connection can be done with three.

For example, Tony Thornton is the editor of eight magazines in Cumbria, England. He wanted to publish an interesting article about the early twentieth-century American composer Harry Woods ("Try a Little Tenderness," "When the Moon Comes Over the Mountain") – but he had no illustrations. He e-mailed one of his American contributors, Eleanor Knowles in San Francisco. She replied that, though she'd never heard of the composer, she did know a man who was very knowledgeable about American popular music. She phoned Bob Grimes who has nearly 80,000 pieces of late nineteenth-/early twentieth-century sheet music, an extensive library of reference books, and a reputation for total recall of everything in his collection.

And did he have a photo of Harry Woods?

"No," replied Grimes thoughtfully. "...I've never seen a photograph of him. Would an *engraved portrait* do?"

Within an hour, that engraved portrait and several beautifully-designed sheet music covers for songs composed by Woods had been scanned and e-mailed directly to England. This "connection" allowed Tony Thornton to illustrate his article lavishly and go to press the next morning.

Don't dismiss your ability to find the information and support you need to pursue your possibilities. An amazing number of people are willing, and even eager, to help others who share their interests and passions. There are five billion potential possibility partners out there, and many are just a few degrees of separation away.

There is nothing on this earth more to be prized than true friendship.

— SAINT THOMAS AQUINAS

4 MULTIPLY YOUR POSSIBILITIES

Who will help you?

WHAT IS A POSSIBILITY PARTNER?

Even the Lone Ranger was not alone. I find it fascinating that an American icon who was revered for courage and justice found strength in partnership. The name "Lone Ranger" suggests a solitary existence. However, his partner, Tonto, was an integral part of his success. We all need to have Tontos and *be* Tontos. We all need *possibility partners*.

I love the Japanese proverb, "No one of us is as smart as all of us." Isn't that true? No single person knows everything. We need others to accelerate our learning curve so that we can rise above our current level of performance. Many successful people I've met tell me they have achieved what they previously thought was impossible by finding, developing, or creating possibility partners. These advisers allow them to access new wisdom, new perspectives, and new *possibilities*.

Peak performers quickly acknowledge that their own thinking may not be enough. If we are to excel, we need others to exchange ideas with, people who encourage our vision, excite our thinking, challenge us, and equip us with tools. These wonderful people can provide much needed support and encouragement as we strive to achieve our purpose.

Encouragers can inspire us to act boldly in spite of our circumstances. They remind us that setbacks are temporary and future possibilities are within our grasp. They provide reality checks without destroying dreams.

Who are these encouragers, these possibility partners? They are all around us. A possibility partner doesn't have to be a CEO, a celebrity, or a person of great power or wealth. They very likely can be someone who others regard as "ordinary" and therefore over-looked. Potential possibility partners could be:

- Friends and family

- Someone we work with

- Someone who does what we do (for fun or for a living)

- Someone whose interests interconnect in some way with our own

- Teachers

- Role models

- Mentors

- Mentorees

- Experts

- Acquaintances

- Anyone we regularly interact with (bus drivers, store clerks, delivery people)

- Friends of friends

- Total strangers

Possibility partners encourage and guide us in achieving our goals. They try to expand our options by helping us look beyond our current vision. Goals can be calculated and unemotional, but dreaming about them isn't, and it's the dreaming that fuels our possibilities. It is invaluable to have others kindle this passion by encouraging us to see what could be. My own life changed the day I *finally* realized a principle was absolutely true that someone had reminded me of: we can all learn something from everyone!

So, what can possibility partners do for you? Well, they have the potential to:

- Guide you through difficulties.

- Provide encouragement when discouragement sets in.

- Help define and redefine purpose, potential, and possibilities.

- Keep you focused on what's important.

- Motivate you to face anxiety and break through self-imposed barriers.

- Create synergy that will accelerate growth.

- Add new thoughts and new resources.

How do you cultivate "possibility partners"? Here are some guidelines that have proven useful in my life when I needed encouragement.

Go where your partner might be. Fish rarely jump in the boat. It takes some planning and research. Some possibility partners *do* appear serendipitously, but don't count on it. Be proactive. Establish a deliberate course of action to find a suitable partner. Be sure to look for a person who exemplifies your own values.

Seek guidance instead of answers. Possibility partners can offer a different perspective and offer encouragement, walking alongside you. Consider the example of the Sherpa guides who assist visiting mountain climbers on Mt. Everest. They provide direction, tactics, motivation, and, if necessary, oxygen. However, ultimately it is up to the climber to reach the pinnacle. We all need a possibility Sherpa!

Be clear. Identify your challenges and future desires for your potential possibility partner. Most likely, he or she is busy. Be clear about who you are and where you want to be. It gives the relationship a head start.

Think win/win. The most powerful possibility partner relationship is one where *both* develop talents and awareness. Both should benefit from this relationship. To paraphrase President John F. Kennedy, "Don't just ask what they can do for you; ask also what you can do for them."

Of course, some common sense and knowledge of human nature should be used in the selection process. Occasionally, a potential partner will not take the relationship seriously and instead use it as an opportunity to play a practical joke! I recall someone starting out in the speaking business asked the advice of a more experienced speaker (a humorist). He was told he would grab the attention of meeting planners if he bleeped some words in the opening minute of his demo tape, making it appear that he used profanity in his presentations! Ironically, this created unexpected possibilities. He did not enjoy much success as a speaker; however, he became a wildly-successful rap star!

Possibility partners usually fall into three general categories, each useful for multiplying your effectiveness and securing the information and support you need to achieve your possibilities.

Mentors: Those who will support, inspire, and guide you, sharing their expertise. These people can be colleagues, superiors, *and* subordinates.

Mentorees: Those *you* can support, inspire, and guide, sharing your own expertise. You mentor others while learning from them in return.

Subcontractors: Those who will do the parts of the job you can't do or can't do well. This frees you up to do what you do best.

We're going to explore all three categories in this chapter. You are probably already familiar with mentoring and being mentored, a highly rewarding two-way street. There's a saying, "Good teachers learn from their students." When I go to speak to a group, sharing my "wisdom" with them, I nearly always come away with new insights and understanding. What an education I'm getting!

Sharing life experiences allows others to learn from mistakes, without making them, and to evaluate actions, without taking them. A Tonto helps others see possibilities and multiply possibilities that were previously invisible.

If one advances confidently in the direction of his dreams, and endeavors to live the life which he imagined, he will meet with a success unexpected in common hours. He will pass an invincible boundary; new, universal, and more liberal laws will begin to establish themselves around and within him...and he will live with the license of a higher order of beings.

— HENRY DAVID THOREAU

FAMILY AND FRIENDS:
A RUNNING START

Do you remember the first day you rode a bike without training wheels? A friend or family member was most likely there to assist and encourage. They were hanging on to you, and you were hanging on to the bike, and something wonderful was happening. Your mind probably raced with different possibilities. If you're like me, the potential outcomes ranged from popping a wheelie that would be the envy of all the kids to taking a header and having an asphalt sandwich for lunch. At the same time you were learning a valuable lesson about depending on others, you were also experiencing an incredible sense of freedom.

Who doesn't remember the thrill of pedaling a bike for the first time, all by themselves? Remember the scene in the movie *E.T.* where the kids are trying to rescue the alien, and as they are being pursued, their bikes leave the ground and fly through the air? That's how it felt when I was able to ride my bike for the first time. If we are going to multiply our possibilities, we need the people closest to us to "hang on," "cheer us on," and let us soar with a new-found freedom.

Childhood memories, in addition to reminding us of the importance of persistence (and how we can learn from our skinned knees), also remind us of how important emotional and physical support is from others. People closest to you when you were young can become possibility partners. That vital support from family and friends is still available to us as adults; it's often just as important to us now, as we try new things and work through new and exciting challenges. Sharing childhood memories with your possibility partner can also be a lot of fun, so seek out those closest to you!

Our families are a remarkable resource – one that we can all draw on. And here's the really intriguing thing. Not everyone comes from a great family. If you grew up in a negative one, or even had no family at all, it is *still* a resource. Here's why.

Psychologists have long noted that people can have a very negative experience and still retain a positive self-image and outlook for the future. They call this "framing." Two people may have an identical experience but interpret it very differently, drawing diverse conclusions. One "frames" it positively, the other negatively. Thus, a child who has had very poor parenting could decide, "Obviously, I am worthless and undeserving of love," or "People hurt me and cannot be trusted." Alternatively, that child could use positive framing and decide, "My parents were deeply flawed people who taught me what *not* to do in life. Because of them, I am a stronger, more compassionate, resilient person."

A British researcher, David B.P. Sims, analyzed the autobiographies of five successful industrial managers to see if he could identify any common childhood experiences. His unexpected finding was that these five managers had very different backgrounds and shared only one characteristic: all had chosen careers in areas that had little relation to the cultures they had grown up in. Each believed that it was this *discrepancy* that increased his awareness of, and sensitivity to, the lessons learned as a child. All agreed that their early experiences, so different from their later lives, had prepared them for the company, industry, or culture in which they became successful.

I have heard numerous stories that fall into a similar pattern. Two male siblings grew up in the same household but had completely different adult experiences. Their parents were unethical, unloving, and unreliable.

One brother follows the exact path his parents had modeled. Falling short of his potential, he is unsuccessful both personally and professionally. His life is one problem after another.

The other brother uses positive framing and decides *not* to model after his parents. He excels both socially and academically. He lives a life of success and significance, enjoying a loving home life. His life is filled with one possibility after another.

When these two siblings were asked why their lives turned out this way, ironically they gave the same answer. "How could I be any different with parents like mine?"

How your life turns out is not the result of the family you were born into or the experiences you shared. It's what you *learn* from your family that determines whether or not you'll be open to opportunities to multiply your possibilities.

A successful man is one who can lay a firm foundation with the bricks others have thrown at him.

— DAVID BRINKLEY
AMERICAN TV NEWSCASTER

WATT'S UP?

If you doubt the power of possibility, consider what turning on the lights can do.

Let me start by saying that I am a die-hard Cleveland sports fan. If you don't follow professional sports, you wouldn't know that Cleveland has not had a world championship in any sport since 1960. Nevertheless, their stadiums sell out, and their citizens still believe the team will win. I grew up there and have had the privilege of sitting in the "dog pound" at the stadium during a Cleveland Browns game. Let me set the scene: fans drinking beer, temperature below zero, and everyone donning dog masks and yelping for their beloved Browns. It was culture shock to attend a San Francisco 49ers game where no one barked and, instead of beer and brats, there was chardonnay and paté.

Cleveland is a city that has recently realized its possibilities and now enjoys a renaissance some thought impossible. For years, this city suffered the fate of others in the "rust belt." Many factories shut down. Dilapidated buildings and antiquated infrastructure caused a population shift to the suburbs. The city became a ghost town after 5 PM.

Today, Cleveland is thriving again, with new construction and a bustling downtown. It has been transformed from the "mistake" on the lake to "magnificence" on the lake. How did this happen?

On one of my trips there, I had the privilege of speaking before the Cleveland Rotary Club. When I saw the brand-new warehouse district, baseball stadium, football stadium, sparkling hotels, and the Rock-and-Roll Hall of Fame, I was astounded! I assumed this had all been a masterful plan executed by an expert in city revitalization.

Remarkably, when I asked how this amazing turnaround had been engineered, everyone gave the same answer: "They turned on the lights."

"What lights?" I asked.

"Terminal Tower," they said.

The Terminal Tower building is the *grande dame* of the Cleveland skyline. During the decline of the city, the lights were dimmed at night and eventually turned off. What had once been a beacon of activity now communicated the message that no one was home. The Cleveland Rotarians shared with me that, once the lights were turned on again, everyone's attitude changed dramatically. People were intrigued. What was happening in the city? They wanted to go see. Of course, there were plans for renewal that followed, but if you ask anyone in Cleveland what the *tipping point* was, most would say, "When they lit up the Tower."

Symbols have enormous power. Seeing the Tower lit up made people begin to *think again* that renewal and change were possible. This intriguing sense of possibility motivated many to come together to achieve the "impossible." Possibilities are the foundation of motivation because they give us the reason to act!

We all have periods in our lives when our possibilities need a little revitalization. How do we accomplish this and in turn create more possibilities? Resist getting bogged down in the problems and instead dwell on the possibilities. In other words, focus on the "light" instead of the dark.

A friend of mine recently retired after 40 years as a classroom teacher. I asked him what kept the spark alive to inspire possibilities for himself and others. His answer was simply, "I was a first year teacher 40 times!" Now that's an example of someone who "flipped the switch" on his possibilities.

As a mentor, your job is to *turn on the lights*. Showing you believe in possibilities changes attitudes and helps those possibilities happen. Go ahead and "light up" a life!

For any of us to be truly free-if we are to learn
to soar in this changing world-we must first be
willing to be responsible for our lives. We can
learn to soar only in direct proportion to our
determination to rise above the doubts and
transcend the limitations. We cannot become what
we need to be by remaining what we are.

    — MAX DePREE
    AUTHOR ON LEADERSHIP

BANK ON YOUR POSSIBILITIES

Did you know there's a prize for lending money? Well, not exactly, but Bangladesh economist Muhammad Yunus won the 2006 Nobel Peace Prize for his pioneering work in making small loans to millions of poor people. "He proved the impossible: that the poor were bankable," says Jonathan J. Morduch, an economics professor at New York University. Yunus' loans have been given to destitute widows and abandoned wives, landless laborers and rickshaw drivers, sweepers and beggars.

The Nobel Committee praised Mr. Yunus and the Grameen Bank for making *microcredit*, as the loans are called, a practical solution to combating rural poverty in Bangladesh and for inspiring similar ventures across the developing world. When the committee announced the prize, they stated, "Microcredit has proven to be an important liberating force in societies where women, in particular, have to struggle against repressive social and economic conditions."

Mr. Yunus is a long-time champion of the idea that even the most impoverished people have the drive and creativity to build small businesses if they can get the resources—sometimes a loan as small as $12. The borrowers use the money to buy milk-giving cows, or bamboo to craft stools, or yarn to weave into stoles, or incense to sell in stalls—all modest money-making ideas by American standards, but life-changing for the entrepreneurs.

In 1976, Yunus was teaching "elegant theories of economics" at Chittagong University when he reached into his own pocket to make his first loan of $27 to 42 villagers living nearby. The borrowers had no collateral and signed nothing, but they invested the money and repaid him in full. "If you can make so many people that happy with such a small amount of money, why shouldn't you do more of it?" he said.

Yunus' new model of banking for the poor had several unusual features. For example, the Grameen Bank lent only to groups of five people. Thus, peer pressure helped to make sure that each member repaid his or her share. The bank also required borrowers to repay their loans in manageable weekly installments. The average loan from Grameen Bank was $130.

While microcredit loans are hardly a total cure for the misery and hardship of poverty, the Nobel committee noted that "Yunus' long-term vision is to eliminate poverty in the world. That vision cannot be realized by means of microcredit alone. But Muhammad Yunus and Grameen Bank have shown that, in the continuing effort to achieve a cure, microcredit must play a major part." Since Yunus' first loan, microcredit has become one of the most popular antipoverty strategies in the world. According to Microcredit Summit, a nonprofit advocacy group based in Washington. D.C. that Yunus helped found, last year more than 100 million people received small loans from more than 3,100 institutions in 130 countries.

Muhammad Yunus is a mentor on a world scale, starting with a seemingly "impossible dream," and making it come true for millions of people. It is so easy to assume that huge, complex problems require huge, complex solutions. It is exciting when one person comes along with a simple, workable plan that achieves so much.

Possibility thinkers have the potential to not only impact their own life, as Muhammad Yunus demonstrates, but radically change millions of lives. His unwavering belief in others' potential, despite difficult circumstances, proves an important principal for possibility living. Your possibilities are not determined by where you come from; your possibilities are realized by knowing where were *going*. Mr. Yunus provided the resources and road map that led to possibility opportunities; the people added what multiplies possibilities… resiliency. Your investment in possibilities now can also put you on the road to unlimited opportunities in the future.

The highest use of capital is not to make more money, but to make money to do more for the betterment of life.

— HENRY FORD

STANDING TALLER

Sometimes we inspire and motivate others by sharing what we have experienced. Other times, we share what we haven't experienced. Andre Agassi, a child tennis prodigy, left school in the eighth grade to go on the pro tour. He later completed his education through correspondence courses. When Andre decided to give back to his hometown of West Las Vegas, Nevada, a school seemed the logical thing to him.

A labor of love, the Andre Agassi College Preparatory Academy opened in 2001 for 3rd to 5th grades, which are considered the most pivotal period for the future academic success of a child. Students pay no tuition and are selected by lottery. Many are what are considered "at risk" kids. Each year, another grade is added, advancing the initial students, until the school has a full twelve-year program. Agassi guarantees each graduate a college education.

By its sixth school year, the $4.4 million charter school offered kindergarten through 10th grade, with an enrollment of 530 in classes no larger than twenty-five students. "You wouldn't believe how much has changed there," Agassi says. "There's so much pride. They're getting rid of the graffiti. The respect for the community has grown so much. We've driven in the point that the way to reach a child is through education. But these kids aren't going there simply to stay in school. They're going there because a lot of people are expecting a lot out of them."

Agassi himself pays all the fund-raising expenses of the Andre Agassi Charitable Foundation so that donations—reportedly more than $14 million since 1995—go entirely to the school. But his support is not strictly monetary. He also drops by the school twenty-five to thirty times a year, often unannounced. However, he is not into self-publicity. If Agassi had his choice, he'd take his name off the building. "But he realizes the importance of it for funding the school in perpetuity," says Roy Parker, principal for the elementary and middle schools. "If he had his druthers, it would just be a charter school. This is a selfless undertaking for him...it is his devotion."

"It's about getting fifty kids off to college each year," says Board of Trustees member Bill Hornbuckle, "and keeping it going. It's a massive project, a massive responsibility. It's a great burden. You can't walk away from it. It's far more intricate and emotional. It is forever."

Parents, teachers, and students all sign a "commitment to excellence" contract. Elementary school parents must promise to read daily to their children. All parents must commit to volunteering twelve hours every year at the school. And each child must memorize and recite the school's code of conduct, which is posted inside the front door:

- The essence of good discipline is respect,

- Respect for authority and respect for others,

- Respect for self and respect for rules.

It is an attitude which begins at home, is reinforced at school and then applied throughout life.

"People are going to know who you *are* here," Principal Parker says. No anonymous dropouts here. These kids are going to *be* somebody.

And Andre Agassi explains what this mentoring has meant to him: "Every year, you see these children...all of a sudden, they're ninth graders. You think, 'You were third graders. Look at you. You're standing taller than I am, speaking better than I speak, having more of a plan for your life than I have for mine.' The kids are the best part of this."

When I read the Academy code of conduct, it revealed an important principal of multiplying possibilities. Respecting ourselves increases our expectations for our future. Self-respect is seeing your value and worth. When you don't respect yourself, you live life as a victim of circumstances rather than a creator of opportunities. Embrace this attitude and you, like those in Andre's school, can overcome circumstances that lead to a victorious life!

WHAT A SINGING PIG TAUGHT ME

Anyone who has achieved multiplied possibilities has had colossal flops! Has anyone ever told you that when you make a mistake, put it behind you? Here's what I've learned: put mistakes in front of you and learn everything you can from the experience!

You may have heard of Pat Williams from his days as General Manager of the NBA Philadelphia 76ers and the Orlando Magic. He gained the reputation as a creative genius in promoting his basketball teams, changing the way others think about possibilities. But not every idea paid off the way he hoped it would.

One memorable event was called the Blind Date Night. Male participants were given odd numbered seats while females were given even numbered seats next to the men, creating a blind date for the couples sitting next to each other. The men thought this was great. Fifty-six of them turned out, but only four women showed up. Not a success.

Pat also tried a promotion where fans were challenged to grapple with Victor the Wrestling Bear between the games of a rare doubleheader. Participants' enthusiasm quickly waned when it was discovered that the bear was both toothless and declawed. Not a success.

Then Pat invited Chick the Singing Pig to perform at a game. The swine waddled out to center court, managed an off-key oink, and relieved himself on the floor. The fans would not let this one pass without making their disapproval known. The following day the newspaper read, "Knicks Whip 76ers – Pig Booed." Definitely not a success.

But Pat Williams is a true possibility thinker. Even after such missteps, he persevered and became one of the most respected innovators in professional sports.

Consider this thought: I want you to fail your way to achievement. Now, that may sound contrary to popular motivational advice, but I believe that failure – big, embarrassing fall-on-your-face blunders and bloopers – is invaluable for your future. The experience of failing, failing again, and finally succeeding is the foundation for maximum achievement. If you ask objective self-observers, you will find they have *failed* their way to success. I remember our tennis coach advising, "Fail and fail fast." In other words, identify what does not work, grow from it, and move forward.

John Maxwell honored me by featuring me his book *Failing Forward*. What a great word picture that title is. Every time you fail, you move closer to your objective. Every defeat is providing you valuable information about your action and attitude. With that data, you can reevaluate, reenergize, and recommit to your possibilities.

If you want to experience a power surge of motivation, here is a thought: Remove the word "failure" from your vocabulary. Replace it with "setback," "learning experience," or "trial run." Watch how your energy expands and your enthusiasm explodes when you use these phrases. You erase anxiety and replace it with the anticipation of future possibilities.

INSPIRING CONFIDENCE:
TWO HANDS WORKING

What if you had a workforce where over sixty percent of your employees had disabilities and many had never held jobs before? Could you compete with other businesses? If you said, "No way," *think again*. Just ask Michael Ziegler and a group of parents who once had a powerful vision.

Pride Industries is an organization built on identifying possibilities. It began in 1966 when a group of parents gathered in the basement of St. Luke's Church in Auburn, California, to brainstorm what they could do to create better lives and opportunities for their physically or mentally-challenged children. If anyone had predicted their efforts would result in an organization that is now the world's largest employer of people with disabilities, many would have said, "That's impossible."

Today, Pride Industries is a $100 million business spread across eleven states that employs more than 4,300 people, 2,700 of whom have some type of "handicap." Pride is led by a remarkable leader, Michael Ziegler, who became CEO in 1983 when the organization had 65 employees and $250,000 in annual sales. Mike is the most passionate individual I have ever met. He has an entrepreneurial vision and, most important, he wants to create new possibilities for people with disabilities. He is a "hug-a-minute" kind of guy with an unforgettable and all-encompassing embrace. When I spoke for his organization,

171

I said, "You've heard of a bear hug. Well, Mike gives you a *griz-zly* bear hug, but one with a positive attitude."

Pride Industries is now a thriving, self-sufficient company. It has a clear mission statement: Provide jobs for people with disabilities. Mike says he is so proud that everyone gets a paycheck and that many employees have gone from receiving taxpayers' assistance to being taxpayers.

One of the most memorable experiences of my life was when Mike took me on a tour of his company. Most people would have regarded many of the individuals I saw as unemployable. Yet, there they were, contributing to the success of this company. When they saw Mike, they got in line for a hug and a word of encouragement. What struck me was that Mike knew their names and something about each of them.

There are four core lines of business at Pride Industries: facility support services, government services, mail and fulfillment services, and manufacturing and logistics services. It has contracts with companies like Intel, Microsoft, and General Motors. It is an organization built on finding possibilities in others, no matter what their circumstances. Michael Ziegler refuses to let this be a token button-sorting kind of job. He wants all the employees to *earn* their paychecks, increasing their self-respect in the process. The supervisors skillfully identify what abilities each employee has and uses them effectively.

One thing I saw inspires me to this day. There were two men with cerebral palsy. Each had the use of only one arm. They had put their wheel chairs side by side and, with one using his left hand and the other using his right hand, the two were assembling gift boxes of Jelly Belly candy!

Mike told me that many people might look at the circumstances of some of his employees and ask, "How could *they* be gifted?" "We ask a *different* question," he said. "*How* are they gifted? When we find the answer and place them in an appropriate job, their lives and possibilities expand enormously."

Michael Ziegler offers us an important principle for multiplying possibilities and effective living. We change our possibilities when we change the questions we ask. And when we ask the *right* questions, we can create possibilities for others.

Disability is a matter of perception. If you can do just one thing well, you're needed by someone.

— MARTINA NAVRATILOVA
FORMER WORLD NO. 1
FEMALE TENNIS PLAYER

HAVE YOU KISSED YOUR ASHTRAY TODAY?

How do you get people to stop drinking, smoking, eating junk food, and engaging in other self-destructive behaviors? Well, obviously not by telling them how bad it is and how weak they are because they can't kick these habits. And not by scaring and threatening them.

Throughout history, such authoritarian approaches have rarely worked, although this hasn't stopped the powers that be from trying. Public health service advertising continues to warn us about heart attacks, strokes, and diabetes; pregnant women are cautioned that drinking may cause Fetal Alcohol Syndrome; and cigarette packs display skulls and crossbones on their labels. But few people are sufficiently influenced by these admonishments to actually curtail their addictions.

However, someone with a different approach to inspiring positive change is Dr. Dean Ornish, Clinical Professor of Medicine at the University of California, San Francisco. Dr. Ornish is widely known for his research on controlling coronary artery disease and campaigning for healthful lifestyle changes that include a low-fat vegetarian diet, no smoking, and regular exercise. To inspire people to make positive changes in their lives, especially when thorny health issues are involved, Dr. Ornish believes that short-term gains are much more motivating to people than the fear of dying.

175

He has suggested possibilities to millions of people he will never even meet by finding an effective way to inspire them to make positive changes in their lives. "As health professionals," he says, "we often talk about risk factors or offer prevention tips, but most patients think those are really boring. And telling patients 'If you don't change your diet or quit smoking you are going to have a heart attack' is not that motivating in the long run. It's too distressing to think about—so they don't. When someone has had a heart attack, they will do anything you tell them for about a month or two. Then the denial comes back and they return to their old patterns because thinking long-term about health crises is just too scary."

Dr. Ornish thinks that appealing to vanity and pointing out immediate possibilites may work much better. For example, instead of "Smoking causes heart disease, emphysema, and lung cancer" a more effective advertising slogan has turned out to be, "Do your kisses taste like licking an ashtray?" Think that ad increases the possibility of more kissing if you quit smoking? You bet!

"That places the consequences of behaviors in the here and now—in present tense," he says. "And people are always making changes and choices when they see immediate benefits. That's the point. Every day, people are out there making monumentally difficult changes in lifestyle—when they have a child, for example, or when they change jobs—but they do it because it is worth it. My observation has been that for many people, a big change to quit smoking is worth making, not only because it can help them live longer, but also because it can help them live better."

Through his extensive writings, Dr. Ornish's common sense advocacy for better health practices has created possibilities and made a difference in the lives of countless people. Inspiring them to make positive changes in their lives has made him a mentor to millions. The message is clear: the promise of possibilities is far more motivating than potential problems. *Think again* and multiply your possibilities by dwelling on the benefits instead of the barriers.

Faith and prayer are the vitamins of the soul;
man cannot live in health without them.

— MAHALIA JACKSON
GOSPEL SINGER

INSPIRING EMPLOYEES

Have you ever wanted to help someone in distress and had your support refused? Did that experience sour your magnanimous spirit? Or did it inspire you to seek new possibilities for generosity?

In the best-selling book *Halftime*, author Bob Buford encourages readers to move beyond success and strive for significance. He says true success is moving beyond your own self-interest and creating possibilities for others. Since I am at the "halftime" of my life, this philosophy has a profound impact on how I think about achievement. As I looked at the people I admire who epitomize providing possibilities for others, the first person who came to mind was Dave Lucchetti.

After floods devastated northern California in 1986, thousands of homeowners wanted to return to their damaged homes but lacked the money to make the necessary repairs. Jim Miller, a salesman for Pabco Gypsum, approached Pabco's parent company, Pacific Coast Building Products, about the possibility of donating wallboard. Because giving back to the community is a tradition at Pacific Coast, President and CEO Dave Lucchetti responded enthusiastically.

Only, it wasn't that easy. All the charitable organizations they initially contacted turned them down, saying they had no methods to qualify recipients for the wallboard and distribute the donation. At this point, most companies would have just dropped the offer, but the staff at Pacific Coast persisted. They finally found a church and then a fraternal organization that agreed to screen applicants and handle the distribution. Within a few days, five truckloads were delivered to the victims in two communities and, soon after, two other disaster areas received more donated wallboard from Pacific Coast.

"For years, I've watched Pacific Coast employees go above and beyond, with selfless sharing at the top of the list," says Lucchetti. Possibility thinking is a mandate throughout the company, and employees have suggested and participated in dozens of projects. Over the years, Pacific Coast employees have taken part in efforts including an annual Paint the Town Project (which provides painting and roofing to low-income homeowners), a holiday season Adopt-a-Family program, Habitat for Humanity, and Susan G. Komen walk to cure cancer. Employees have also lent their support to art programs, fund-raising events, food banks, recycling projects, and environmental concerns. And again, after more California flooding in 1995, Pacific Coast distributed donations of building materials, this time through the Red Cross.

Of course, any company that has survived for more than fifty years has had to do a lot of possibility thinking. Few companies face more challenges than those in the building industry. Both demand and supply alternately skyrocket and flatline in unpredictable cycles depending on the economy, demographic shifts, and random political, meteorological, and social variables. The nimble footwork needed to stay afloat could be compared to that of an old-time lumberjack dancing atop a rolling log on a rushing river.

Pacific Coast started modestly. In 1953, Fred Anderson and his wife, Pat, sold their car and put everything they owned into starting a small, family-owned lumberyard in Sacramento, California. In 1971, Dave Lucchetti started as a "yard man," cutting and loading lumber for customers. Just eight years later he became company president.

What started as a small lumberyard in 1953 has diversified and expanded to offer a wide range of products and services for builders and the construction industry? By being open to possibilities, Fred Anderson and Dave Lucchetti have built a business that now operates in ten states, employs more than 3,400 people, and does $900-million in annual business, frequently expanding into new products and services.

A lot of possibilities had to be considered along the way, and the company's expansion has had as many "downs" as "ups." For example, one of their divisions was acquired when a customer couldn't pay its bill and offered to turn over its contracting business in exchange for what it owed. That was a unique opportunity. Was it the right step toward what Pacific Coast wanted to become? Or could it prove disastrous?

Pacific Coast decided to go for it. Unfortunately, their bank foresaw doom and pulled their line of credit, demanding payment in full—$750,000! "On top of that," recalls Dave, "our large volume of business strained our cash flow nearly to the breaking point. Bankruptcy was a distinct possibility."

To get enough cash to pay bills on time, Dave, Fred Anderson, and others made daily rounds to pick up customers' checks and rush them to the bank, hoping the deposits would keep their own checks from bouncing. "I spent an awful lot of time doing this," Dave says. "Once I walked into the bank with several hundred thousand dollars in checks, just before closing. The poor teller didn't know what to do with them, but we had to get them in that day." The crisis dragged on for months, but eventually their hard work and vision paid off.

"We have taken advantage of opportunities as they presented themselves," Dave told me. "We looked for business that fit with what we were doing. After all these years of expansion, all of our businesses continue to be related."

That last point is important. Pacific Coast Building Products has survived and thrived both by being open to possibilities and by pursuing *only* those that would contribute to their vision of interrelated products and services. The company is now a network of semi-independent enterprises, serving their customers, employees, and communities.

I have been fortunate to call Dave Lucchetti a friend for over 20 years. The generosity of his time and talent has been an inspiration to me. Dave's example of attaining both success and significance has taught me the true meaning of achievement. When you are tempted by all the wonderful possibilities around you, remember to choose the ones that contribute to *your* vision of your goals. Be sure to *think again* about what you should pursue that will bring fulfillment, meaning, and purpose in your life. And a life well lived is not attained by only creating possibilities for ourselves; it is in helping others realize their possibilities too!

I feel the capacity to care is the thing which gives life its deepest significance.

— PABLO CASALS
SPANISH MUSICIAN

STRENGTH IN NUMBERS

You know the cliché, "Don't put all your eggs in one basket." I believe you *should*. Like hunting for Easter eggs, find your personal gifts – what you're really good at and love doing – and then focus all your energy on refining the "eggs" in your basket. You'll achieve a lot more and be a lot happier.

No one is brilliant at everything. Have you ever heard someone say, "Oh, I could never do that because…"? Sometimes it's just because the person lacks one of the several skills needed to achieve the desired result. To increase your possibilities, have you ever thought about *subcontracting* to obtain the skills that you just don't have?

Suppose you're right in the middle of a household project, and you're in need of just the right tool. You dig through your toolbox. There are a couple of tools that resemble what you need, but none is quite right. You have needle nose pliers, but you need a vise grip. If you're like me, you run over to a neighbor who seems to have every tool known to man. Now you're able to finish the job.

Life is like that. You begin an ambitious project, make the necessary plans, and gather what you think you need. However, part way through the project, you realize a vital tool or talent is missing. After struggling with the wrong tool, have you ever noticed how useful "the right tool" becomes?

This is the great benefit of having possibility partners with a variety of tools, many of which you do not possess. Your repertoire and available options expand enormously until you've got more specialty tools than the *Yankee Workshop* and just as much expertise to get the job done. You're no longer faced with trying to use a hammer as a screwdriver.

Take a few moments to think about what "tools" you have and what you might need to achieve your possibilities. Develop possibility partners who will share their tools with you, just as you share yours with them.

In the old days, people looked for business partners (and life partners) who could supply the talents they lacked. One person would be a great people person, greeting customers and motivating staff, while the other was skilled at handling finances and business matters. Or one would be a great designer and the other a dynamite marketer. One might be excellent at seeing the big picture, but poor at details, while the other was just the opposite. Each person complemented the other to create a whole greater than the sum of the parts.

Most large projects use *subcontracting*. Businesses and even countries devote their energies to doing what they do best and then fill in the blanks with outside services. You can do the same!

Suppose your goal is to photograph iron bridges in Europe, but you're weak at plotting itineraries, reading timetables, and booking reservations. Then subcontract the travel arrangements portion of your project. You'd go to an experienced travel agent or get a traveling companion to handle this for you, so you could concentrate on what you want to do and what you do well. What if you need the bridge photos for a book you've written, but you don't know one end of a camera from the other. Subcontract that part of your project to a skilled photographer. Making travel arrangements is a piece of cake for you, but languages are difficult. You could hire a translator or team up with a buddy who has that skill.

Consider some talent and weakness combinations that might be parlayed into possibilities:

- You're a terrific "people person" but absolutely no good at the day-to-day details of organizing and running a project.

- You're gifted at managing *things*, but your ability to motivate and inspire other *people* is low. You always seem to put your foot in your mouth and alienate others.

- You're very creative, but your time management and budgeting skills are weak.

- You're not the least bit artistic, couldn't tell a Monet from a motet, but doing budgets and taxes is easy for you.

- You're super at puzzles, but...

- Sports – or writing – or speaking – come easily to you, but...

You get the idea. We each have *some* things that we excel at. Identify yours and use them to multiply your possibilities to achieve what you want. As we learned in *Amplify Your*

Possibilities, we all have definite weaknesses too. Identify yours and then learn to *leverage* them—which doesn't mean "overcoming" them; acknowledge your weaknesses and use them as a tool. Turn limitations into strengths by fitting them into your big plan.

If you're not sure how to do this, imagine you are an employer eager to match your employees' skills and experiences to the jobs you want done. What unique niche might someone with your particular profile fill? For example, here's a common characteristic that many people would see as failure. Suppose you have enormous energy for starting new projects, but then your interest drops off and you never finish. How could this "weakness" be turned into strength?

There was a formidable Englishwoman named Rachel Kay-Shuttleworth (1896–1967), who specialized in conceiving and organizing social service and public betterment projects, sort of a British equivalent of Eleanor Roosevelt. Once a project was under way, Rachel would find the right people to take it over, organize and inspire them, and then leave them with a clear road map of where to go. Once this was done, she'd move on to a new project.

Rachel made invaluable contributions to infant and maternal health among the poor, juvenile justice and prison reform, the Girl Guides (British Girl Scouts), education, community services, civic betterment, housing, and social services for World War II evacuees. Her passion for needle arts and crafts resulted in many training programs, and she personally amassed the largest private collection of historic needlework, textiles, and quilts in the world, now housed in a teaching museum in Lancashire, England.

Rachel was so beloved by those whose lives she had touched that, when developers threatened to do open strip-mining near her home and she told them she'd get every Girl Guide in northern England to stand in front of their bulldozers, the developers knew that she could. They retreated, choosing instead to change the course of a nearby river! Thus, throughout her life, this dynamic woman made a virtue of the seeming vice of starting projects that she didn't finish herself.

Unlike Rachel, there are people who can't conceive or create a project but who can become super team builders and follow through long-term once they are motivated and given clear instructions. This might be you or someone you are seeking to motivate and inspire. Again, get around the perceived vice and turn it into a virtue.

You don't have to be talented at everything to achieve great results. Consider multiplying your own abilities by finding others who can do what you don't do well. Whether you pay an expert or team up with others to supplement your deficits, you can often achieve your goals by *subcontracting*. Remember, Michelangelo didn't *build* the Sistine Chapel ceiling. He just painted it!

I dunno, she's got gaps, I got gaps,
and together we fill gaps.

— ROCKY'S RESPONSE WHEN ASKED WHY HE
LIKED ADRIAN (FROM 1976 FILM *ROCKY*)

5

QUANTIFY
YOUR PROGRESS

How will you know when you're there?

THE POWER OF
(IM)POSSIBILITY THINKING

I love to tell a story about the three questions a Canadian border guard asked me when I was returning to the U.S. from a business trip:

- Where are you coming from?

- How long have you been there?

- Where are you going?

These questions triggered my thinking about human potential and inspired me to write *How High Can You Bounce?* One group resistant to this book title was an association of skydivers. It seems they avoid anything with the word bounce in it. More recently, the border questions have changed:

- What is the nature of your trip?

- Do you have anything to declare?

- If so, what is the approximate value?

As you've read this book, you've actually been considering these three questions. You started by defining the nature of your trip – your dreams and your ideal life. Then you thought about any negativity or pessimism that might be blocking your way. Next, you considered your resources, talents, passions, and uniqueness. Then you reflected on the concept of multiplying the resources you need to pursue your possibilities through possibility partners, mentoring, and subcontracting. Now, in Part 5, you'll consider ways to evaluate, extend, and achieve your possibilities.

"Value" has two distinct meanings. Both are essential for pursuing possibilities. We live, with varying degrees of success and comfort, by our *values* – our beliefs and ethics. And we place a *value* on each of the many conflicting fragments of day-to-day living. But some people, as Oscar Wilde commented, can know the price of everything and the value of nothing.

With all the pressures we face every day, it's easy to be distracted from our beliefs and overlook some of our real riches. We are constantly torn between options, confronting choices, and making quick decisions that can have profound effects on our lives. By declaring our values and the value of our choices, we make our lives infinitely richer and more profound. We can focus on attaining and sustaining our essential core, the gift we give ourselves and the world.

It's fairly easy to be grateful for the good things, but even burdens and frustrations can offer positive value if you know how to look for it. What is the value to you of navigating a difficult situation? When you've come through an awkward or painful time, do you feel grumpy and put-upon, asking "Why me?" Or for having made it, do you feel stronger, wiser, and better able to appreciate and enjoy the good things?

190

New wisdom is one of the greatest perks of those less-than-perfect times. How often have you said, "If only I knew then what I know now." Wouldn't it be great to replay your life with the wisdom you now possess? Well, we can't go backwards and do it all over again. But we have an even greater gift. We can move forward with our new wisdom. We can respond with improved judgment, greater knowledge, and more patience and understanding the next time things don't go just the way we'd hoped. With our broader perspective, we can define negative events as glitches instead of catastrophes.

When you come up with your own answer to "What is the value of working through this difficult situation?," you become open to using both the positive and negative experiences of your day with a life-affirming attitude of gratitude. With a grateful mind-set, you constantly re-energize your heart and soul.

A friend of mine likes to say, "We have a choice when we wake up in the morning. We can groan and pull the covers over our head, moaning, 'Oh, God, it's morning!' Or we can rise, greet our loved ones, and gaze out the window at the rain or shine of the glorious planet we live on, and gratefully say, 'Oh, God, it's morning!'"

You increase your personal happiness and achievement when you value whatever makes your life enjoyable and challenging, even the smallest things. Your "attitude of gratitude" makes you even more open to noticing and taking advantage of the wealth of possibilities awaiting you.

As you start your day, take a few seconds to focus on what you truly value. As you quantify your progress and celebrate your success, watch how your gratitude grows.

Empower yourself by celebrating and acknowledging all the good in your life. This is how the seemingly impossible becomes possible.

For a long time it had seemed to me that life was about to begin – real life. But there was always some obstacle in the way, something to be gotten through first, some unfinished business, time still to be served, a debt to be paid. Then life would begin. At last it dawned on me that these obstacles were my life.

— ALFRED D. SOUZA

"IF I EVER DECIDE TO WORRY"

As I registered at the reception desk, a young man in military uniform greeted me with a smart salute and handshake. The bustling activity and energy all around us was unforgettable. I wish you could have been there with me.

We were standing at the entrance to Walter Reed Army Medical Center in Washington, D.C. I had been invited to give my presentation called "Challenges are Inevitable – Defeat is Optional" to a group of injured military personnel returning from Iraq and Afghanistan. To be invited to speak to these soldiers was a tremendous privilege, especially for a civilian. I felt both honored and humble, uncertain whether what I had to say would be relevant to these people who had faced so many challenges already.

My escort informed me that he would be my guide for the day. I was to stick with him and not go anywhere unescorted during my visit. As we walked through the rotunda, I thought about all the sick and injured that had been treated here, everyone from buck privates to presidents. The walls were covered with large paintings of famous military leaders, their expressions conveying strength and patriotism.

We went first to meet the Chief of Staff, who also greeted me with a firm handshake. He presented me with a cherished memento, a military medallion that signifies courage. During our conversation, he informed me that several soldiers would be unable to attend my presentation due to their injuries, but they had asked that I visit them in their rooms afterward. Before my arrival, I had sent along autographed copies of my book *How High Can You Bounce?* and many had already read it.

Then I was led into the main auditorium for my formal presentation. When those large doors swung open, I will never forget what I saw. Although I pride myself on showing up early to prepare, there were already two-hundred young men and woman waiting for me. My initial surprise was that the audience wasn't all male. My second surprise was seeing how young they all were. I think of myself as a young man, yet many of them could have been my sons or daughters.

My escort introduced me to the group, and I began my speech. As I looked at the faces of these heroes, a young man to my right caught my attention. He had a great big magnetic smile, a grin so engaging that I didn't realize immediately that both his arms had been amputated at the elbow and that his right leg was missing. Next to him was a woman who, I assumed, was on staff at Walter Reed.

At the completion of my talk, this woman began to clap loudly – so loudly that I was somewhat embarrassed. I felt *I* was the one who should have been applauding everyone in this group. I walked over to her and said how much I appreciated her positive response.

"Roger," she said, "my son asked me to applaud extra loudly for him. He won't be clapping anytime soon." And she nodded toward the young man in the wheelchair. Fighting back tears, I realized this soldier was her child.

I went over to talk to him, kneeling down so I would be eye-level with him. He eagerly shared his plans for his life with me. "Tell me," I finally asked, "where does your courage come from?"

Gesturing with the stumps of his arms, he said, "Roger, I can't wait to see what I can do with this." Adding with a mischievous grin, "At first, I was really down and discouraged, but then I realized there was a bright side. If I ever decide to worry about the future, I won't be able to bite my nails!"

The word courage comes from the Latin word cor, which means heart. Do people with incredible courage just have a heart that does not feel fear? I don't think so! Courage is not discovered; courage is a decision.

You have been my friend. That in itself is a tremendous thing. I wove my webs for you because I liked you. After all, what's a life, anyway? We're born, we live a little while, and we die. A spider's life can't help being something of a mess, with all this trapping and eating flies. By helping you, perhaps I was trying to lift up my life a trifle. Heaven knows anyone's life can stand a little of that.

— CHARLOTTE
FROM *CHARLOTTE'S WEB*

Courage is not the absence of fear,
but rather the judgment that something
else is more important than fear.

— AMBROSE REDMOON

Courage is resistance to fear, mastery
of fear – not absence of fear.

— MARK TWAIN

Courage is being scared to death,
but saddling up anyway.

— JOHN WAYNE

HOPING OR HAPPENING?

Once you are well on your way to accomplishing your goals, follow-through is critical to achieving your possibilities. Quantifying and evaluating your progress is the difference between hoping possibilities will work out someday and making possibilities happen. The process helps you identify where you are and serves as a guide to where you want to be. Here is the thinking process.

THE THREE R'S OF QUANTIFYING

Rate where you are. This is reality-based thinking. What are the facts? Have I made the planned-for progress? Am I meeting my benchmarks? Am I taking a global view of my circumstances and a *macro*-look at my possibilities?

Review strategy. Take a *micro*-view of possibilities. What am I excelling at? What still needs work? Do strategic goals need to be redefined? Bring possibility partners into the process. Implement tactics.

Revise. Make any mid-course adjustments needed to advance toward your possibilities. Look for ways to improve and increase efficiency.

"The road to success" is a popular expression, but this image is somewhat misleading. I prefer to think of the way to success as a *path*. When I visualize a *road*, it is relatively smooth and well marked, with identifiable stopping points and speed limits. It is usually well traveled. However, a *path* is typically more difficult to follow. It may be uneven, rocky, meandering, and often desolate. It's easy to stumble and even get lost, and you can go a long way alone without running into another traveler.

Ordinary possibilities may lie at the end of a straight, heavily-trafficked road, but extraordinary possibilities are usually reached by a path. If your journey is challenging, circuitous, and uncertain – often an uphill climb – then extraordinary possibilities may await you.

Security is mostly a superstition. It does not exist in nature, nor do the children of men as a whole experience it. Avoiding danger is no safer in the long run than outright exposure. Life is either a daring adventure or nothing.

— HELEN KELLER

DON'T JUST DO SOMETHING – SIT THERE!

We have a five-pound Pomeranian named Mac-A-Roon who lets *us* live with *him*. His attitude is much more Great Dane than Pom. He is always showing us his doggie tricks, undoubtedly eager to amuse "his people." One of his favorites is to spin in a circle a few times. His reward is a dog biscuit or, as we call it, a cookie.

Soon after we were married, I heard my wife say, "Sweetie, spin if you want a cookie." I mistakenly thought she was talking to me and spun so rapidly that I became lightheaded and collided with the kitchen table. Mac-A-Roon gave me a look that communicated, "You people are so hard to train."

Whenever I watch Mac-A-Roon spin in a circle, I am reminded how often I feel that way – that I am spinning into things and hard to train. Despite my best intentions, I frequently feel overscheduled and stressed – as if I am running on a treadmill and making very little progress.

Do you remember as a child being so swept up in thought that time stood still? I still recall how wonderful that kind of daydreaming felt. It was a peaceful and harmonious state. Or do you remember how it felt to be so focused on a balloon or a bug that everything else around you was totally blurred? I have watched my own daughter drift off into such a trance-like state, and I have caught myself saying something like, "Earth to Alexa..." or "Anybody home?" One reason we continually have to remind our children to stop doing what they're doing and do something else is that they have a tremendous capacity for this kind of focused concentration.

Why does daydreaming often stop as we get older? Why do we lose the ability to be totally captivated by the moment? Why do we stop cultivating our imaginations? I believe it's because we feel guilty. We've been taught that if we take time to dream, engage in imaginary ventures, or just be still, we are somehow neglecting our responsibilities. Over time, our minds become so cluttered with practical things that there is little room left for anything else. We become, as I said previously, "terminally adult."

One of the valuable lessons I have learned from those who achieve great possibilities is that they are all great dreamers. Too often we buy into the myth that possibilities require constant activity with no time for rejuvenation. Our busy-ness erodes our wonder about what's possible. High achievers do not let everyday concerns get in the way of thinking about their possibilities. They intentionally take time to have child-like dreams about *what if?* Have you noticed that children rarely believe something is impossible? Ask them, "What do you want to be when you grow up?" and their answers are often ambitious and exciting. Give yourself time to evaluate your progress. Think again and imagine possibilities.

So long as we believe in our heart of hearts that our capacity is limited and we grow anxious and unhappy, we are lacking in faith. One who truly trusts in God has no right to be anxious about anything.

— PARAMAHANSA YOGANANDA, INDIAN YOGI

ACT WITH IMPACT

Activity is very different from accomplishment. Some people confuse busyness with importance and bustle with impact. People who achieve great possibilities concentrate on doing the most important thing every day, rather than frittering away their time on a hundred other daily demands. They focus on what will yield the greatest benefit.

Here's an acronym that many people respond enthusiastically at my presentations:

I Inspiration occurs when your dreams are so compelling that they wrap around your heart. This is the root of passion.

M Motivation happens when you wrap your mind around your possibilities and decide to take the action necessary to make them a reality. This is where purpose comes into focus.

P Precision. Possibilities require specific planning and preparation. It is in this process that dreams become possibilities.

A Acquisition. Possibilities require that we continue to gain new knowledge and expertise. It is in this process of getting better that our possibilities get better.

C Connection. Possibilities are multiplied when we enlist the energy and encouragement of others. No one does it alone.

T Transformation. Realizing we can do more and become more transforms discouragement into hope. Hope as it strengthens gives us greater courage, which leads to greater possibilities.

Understanding the meaning of impact is obviously not enough to achieve great possibilities. You must also *act* with impact. Here are four things to accomplish that:

FOUR KEYS TO ACTING WITH IMPACT

Get started. Have you ever watched a horse race, and the track announcer cries, "They're off!" Visualize the beginning of your day the same way. Start your activities with a sprint instead of a trot. Commit to possibility-producing activities and concentrate on them single-mindedly, without diversion and distraction. Realize that every minute of every hour is filled with possibility. Develop a sense of urgency toward important activities, and apply the discipline necessary to complete them. Once you've developed the habit of beginning your day in this way, you're off in pursuit of amazing possibilities.

Be a simpleton. Remember the old putdown, "simpleton"? Well, sometimes being "simple" about things is a strength instead of a weakness. Being able to simplify one's life and work is an invaluable skill for a possibility producer. I loved the commercial that transformed Fabio from young to old with the tag line, "Life comes at you fast." Isn't that true?

The velocity of change seems to be increasing rapidly. The more change, the more possibilities, but it is a double-edged sword. The solution is to discontinue tasks that move you away from possibilities. When you reduce low-value activities, you produce peak performance. Earlier, you read about the power of subcontracting some tasks as a way to leverage your strengths. It is also helpful to *eliminate* some of the tasks that you are not particularly skilled in.

Affect your effectiveness. An employee asks his boss, "When will my raise be effective?" His boss responds, "When *you* are!" To act with impact requires maximum effectiveness. Focus on those things you can control. Try to improve every day. Decide to be a perpetual student, always eager for new knowledge and experiences. Dorothy Fuldheim was a newscaster in Cleveland, Ohio for decades. In her nineties, she signed a five-year contract and was asked afterwards when she planned to retire. "When I'm old," she replied.

Focus on solutions. I was watching a morning TV show featuring an expert instructing viewers on winter driving. "When you encounter slippery conditions," the expert said, "steer away from the problem and toward the solution." Life is the same. As you navigate treacherous circumstances, resist concentrating on the problems. Focus on the possibilities – on where you want to end up. The more you dwell on possibilities, the more creative you become at solutions. If you are tempted to focus on difficulties – on where you don't want to go – then the fruit of your mindset will be disappointment and pessimism.

If you steer toward solutions, then inspiration and creativity will be the products of your focus.

Every day there are hundreds of demands, large and small, on our limited time, energy, and resources. If we try to do everything, our most important core goals may get lost in the shuffle.

Identify your high-value activities—those that will have the most impact on achieving your possibilities and goals—and focus on them. Learn to act with impact.

Difficult times have helped me to understand better than before, how infinitely rich and beautiful life is in every way, and that so many things that one goes worrying about are of no importance whatsoever...

— ISAK DINESEN
DANISH AUTHOR

PERFECT TIMING?

"If your ship does not come in," my dear friend Cavett Robert used to say, "start swimming." What a great metaphor for taking action now, no matter what the circumstances. People who, as we say in tennis, "rip it," don't paralyze themselves with endless and repetitive analyzing, organizing, or contemplating. Of course they have a plan, but once they have established their target and route, they move into action mode. They run into the inevitable obstacles, even failures, but they keep going.

So often, we buy into the myth of "perfect timing." Yes, timing is absolutely essential for comedy, cooking, and conversation. Split-seconds count in things like nuclear fission, space launches, and air traffic control. Even Shakespeare wrote about the importance of timing as "a tide in the affairs of men," which had to be gauged carefully before success could be possible. Missing high tide to get out of the harbor meant "all the voyage of their life is bound in shallows and in miseries."

Two actions that will help you progress in expanding your possibilities are:

> *Choose your pain.* No one wants to hurt, but pain is
> an inevitable part of our lives. Sometimes our only
> choice is how and when we want to hurt. This

became clear to me when my valued friend, Nido Qubein, said, "We choose between the pain of taking action and the pain of regret." Whenever I'm debating a course of action, I remember his words. Invariably, my decision is to "rip it"!

Concentrate on what you procrastinate. All of us delay *something!* Procrastinate the unimportant activities that produce little or no results. Take action on the possibility producing activities that move you closer to your ultimate objective!

Hindsight reveals that there is rarely an ideal time to start your life's mission. Waiting, postponing, and procrastinating are the saboteurs of possibilities. The most important thing is to *just get going.* How many times have you said, "Someday…"?

Well, today is the day to "rip it." Do not delay. Don't wait for that illusive right moment. Start now. Learn from mistakes. Ask for feedback. Make necessary changes. Keep moving towards your goals. As the Nike Company slogan says, "Just do it!"

While one person hesitates because he feels inferior, another is busy making mistakes and becoming superior.

— HENRY C. LINK
AMERICAN PSYCHOLOGIST

PATIENT? OR PASSIVE?

Sometimes all we want are answers, commitments, and achievements, and we want them now! "It shouldn't take this long," we insist. "Be patient," we are told. "These things take time." Other times, we're all too willing to wait and see what happens... which can be zero. "I held out in this dead-end job until something better came along, but nothing did."

What's the difference between being wisely patient and foolishly passive? How can you tell the difference between expectant waiting and a resigned attitude that tells people, "Nothing good ever happens to me"?

Patience is an active stance, not a passive one. This may seem confusing because most people equate patience with inaction. *Think again!* Being patient means that you have done all you can to prepare, and now things are out of your hands. It's time to sit back and trust that the work you've done will bring the results you want. But if you haven't set things in motion and are still waiting for an outcome, you're just being passive.

> A *passive attitude* means that you continue to wait for what you want, taking no action toward your goal, yet maintaining an attitude that what you want should come your way just because you are waiting.

A patient attitude comes after noticing and selecting a possibility, assessing the goal, planning, marshalling resources and supports, putting the plan in action, and then waiting for results.

What if you want to help your daughter get into the higher reading group at school? You can complain loudly to anyone who will listen that you think she belongs there (passive). Or you can sit down with her and help her improve her reading and vocabulary skills, and then wait for the next regular reading test to be administered (patient).

Have you ever noticed how different children react to being told they need to wait? Two kids want new bikes for summer vacation. They both cut out pictures from magazines and spend hours at the bike shop admiring the bikes. Their parents say, "You have to be *patient*. It takes *time* to earn enough money for a bike, and we really can't afford it *yet*." Notice that the parents have given the children an important clue. "You must be patient and wait" is only half of the message. The second half reveals what is needed: money. One child hears the whole message and takes action, doing odd jobs to earn money toward the purchase, waiting patiently until sufficient funds are accrued. The other child does nothing and waits passively.

Patience following preparation is a virtue. Dag Hammarsjöld, former Secretary General of the United Nations, said it well when he described how his mountaineering skills had prepared him for one of the highest international positions in politics: "Mountaineering calls...for endurance... perseverance and patience, a firm grip on realities, careful but imaginative planning, a clear awareness of the dangers, but also of the fact that fate is what we make it and that the safest climber is he who never questions his ability to overcome difficulties."

Nothing in this world can take the place of persistence. Talent will not; nothing is more common than unsuccessful people with talent. Genius will not; un-rewarded genius is almost a proverb. Education will not; the world is full of educated derelicts. Persistence and determination alone are omnipotent. The slogan 'press on' has solved and always will solve the problems of the human race.

— CALVIN COOLIDGE

WHERE'S YOUR AIR?

Have you ever seen an uninflated volleyball or basketball, one with no air in it? What a sorry sight! When I was a kid, I used to marvel that it was the same air *outside* the ball as *inside* it, but what a difference *location* can make. Moving the air from outside to inside the ball gave it its shape, elasticity, and power.

Remember the old Bill Cosby routine: "Why is there air? To fill up basketballs." I agreed. The concept of breathing and needing air to live, to sustain life, didn't make much sense to me; but the concept of needing air to make a ball be a ball, to make it bounce, made perfect sense. Poke a hole in a basketball, and watch the ball – and the game – disappear. Smash a ping pong ball too hard, and the game is over.

Of course, filling a ball with air isn't a permanent proposition. As it sits in the garage, it will gradually deflate. Even after just a few weeks, it loses much of its bounce. People are the same. Just as we continuously feed our bodies with oxygen, we need to restock our "bounce factor" to nourish our spirits. When our bounce factor is in good shape, we are better able to spot and seize new opportunities, as well as quantify our progress. Get ready to bounce before you need to.

Staying pumped up is a continual process. Start by trying to notice good things every day, no matter how much stress and negativity you run into. It's not always easy, but it's well worth the effort. Each bright, positive moment you notice may offer a possibility. Mentally stockpiling these moments is like creating a reserve of pure oxygen, ready to keep you going toward your goals when your stamina gets low.

Next, to increase your elasticity, work on your attitude toward clearly stressful situations. For example, if someone – a boss, relative, or friend – finds fault with something you've done, listen to the criticism as if it were a gift. Maybe the complaints are valid and useful, maybe not. Try taking the attitude that an appreciative, open mind makes it possible for others to teach you what they know and inform you of their perceptions. Recognize that, if you have an open attitude, your critics may actually become your possibility partners.

Accepting criticism grudgingly is no easier than accepting it gracefully and gratefully. In fact, it's a lot harder. No one enjoys being attacked. Rejecting criticism can make you feel better in the short run because it protects you from admitting you might have something to learn. But *think again.* Does acting defensive really soften the blow? Or would it be better to leverage the energy of the attack, using it to "bounce" you to the next level?

I recommend using the momentum to propel you toward the basket. The person who found fault with you will appreciate your wisdom in acknowledging the complaints, rather than arguing. Except for a few malevolent individuals you'll encounter from time to time, most people would rather praise than condemn. They want things to go smoothly as much as you do.

Delivering criticism requires energy. You can deflect that energy by either lashing back or by bouncing forward. Those seven-foot basketball players can use their jumping ability to push the ball out of bounds, back in the face of the shooter, or toward the basket. Become a winning possibility player by choosing to move toward the goal.

Finally, in the most difficult situations, ask yourself what you have to gain from the experience. Hang on to that nugget of learning. It is pure gold and can open up future possibilities.

Don't pray when it rains if you don't
pray when the sun shines.

— LEROY (SATCHEL) PAIGE
CONSIDERED ONE OF BASEBALL'S
GREATEST PITCHERS

PLAYING TO WIN

During a highly competitive tennis match, as you hover between victory and defeat, the dreaded cement elbow can set in. This happens when you focus on "playing not to lose" instead of "playing to win."

For those of you who don't play tennis, let me describe the condition. It begins when you start responding conservatively, not taking risks. As you do, the net slowly grows taller and your legs begin to turn to rubber. Your mouth feels as if you swallowed a cashmere sweater, and your arm locks up like it's cast in cement.

How do you crack the cement elbow? Like the Nike slogan of "Just do it!" tennis has a saying that conveys the same philosophy: "Grip it, rip it, and forget it." It works like this:

Grip it: Take control of what you can influence. Take the initiative. You cannot control the wind, the sun, or your opponent, so concentrate on what is controllable. Choices can only be made in the present. Don't worry about the last point or the next point. Focus on the present.

Rip it: Take action. Give it maximum effort. Hold nothing back. Lay it on the line. Do not focus on the net (obstacle). Focus on your opponent's open court (possibility). Anticipate success and take your best shot. A victory is made up of hundreds of such shots.

Forget it: Whatever the outcome of the last shot, keep going. Don't spend a second reacting to that miss. Get ready to grip it and rip it again.

This kind of thinking lets you break through anxieties and keep going. Ironically, when you focus on playing rather than winning or losing, you're far more likely to win.

In sports they say there are two types of players: those who play to win and those who play not to lose. Here are the characteristics of the two.

PLAYING NOT TO LOSE

- Cautious

- "Ready...aim...aim...aim"

- Needs reassurance

- Avoids pain at all costs

- Quick to blame

- Risk averse

- Sees obstacles before opportunity

- Looks at failure as final.

PLAYING TO WIN

- Adventurous

- "Ready...aim...fire...fire...fire"

- Believes she or he has what it takes

- Understands that temporary pain
  can equal permanent growth

- 100 percent responsible for attitudes and achievement

- Ready for risk if there is worthwhile reward

- Sees possibilities before problems

- Willing, even eager, to fail, knowing
  this brings success closer.

My close friend and fellow speaker Tony Alessandra grew up in Manhattan's "Hell's Kitchen." One of his favorite expressions is so typically New York: "Fahgetaboutit." This attitude is essential when you are playing to win. A tennis match is comprised of points that are won or lost by the shots you attempt. Some shots are clear winners. Others hit the net. Some shots are picture-perfect, while others are hit so awkwardly that the ball disappears over the fence and is gone for good. Life is a lot like that: a series of events – some memorable, others miserable, some annoying, and some astounding.

In tennis there is a tendency to be so caught up in plans for the next point or in bemoaning a missed shot that you don't pay attention to the present. Tennis coaches have a valuable admonition: "Play in the present." The wisdom is that you let go of the past; and the future is not here yet. All you have to focus on is the current shot. In other words, do not make this shot a rehearsal for an imaginary future performance.

When the "game" is over, then there's time to stop and evaluate how you played and what you could do differently next time. Without analyses of your progress, you may make the same mistakes over and over, never learning from them. In the midst of the process, forget the gain or loss that just happened. Concentrate instead on *making the next shot your best shot*, each and every time. Don't paralyze yourself by thinking how the last shot went or worrying about the difficulty of shots to come. Opportunities to win the game open up for positive possibility thinkers.

There is one quality that one must possess to win, and that is definiteness of purpose, the knowledge of what one wants, and a burning desire to possess it.

— NAPOLEON HILL
AUTHOR OF *THINK AND GROW RICH*

BE LIKE MIKE

You likely remember the commercial that showed Michael Jordan flying through the air completing one of his awe-aspiring dunks and the slogan was "Be Like Mike!" He is arguably the greatest basketball player and most popular athlete in history!

What you may not know is that Michael Jordan ranks number one in only one NBA career statistic! There's a popular notion that successful people do everything well and never experience failure. Michael Jordan is someone who disproves this myth. Not that he wasn't amazingly good. Even non-sports-fans know his name. In fact, Michael Jordan became so recognizable that when one ad showed him in silhouette with no identifying caption, just an outline of his famous bald head, people instantly knew it was "MJ."

To ardent basketball fans like me, he will always be "His Airness." The man seemed to walk on air as he completed jaw-dropping jump shots. Millions of youngsters dreamed of being an NBA superstar, and they all wanted to "be like Mike." Fellow player Magic Johnson said, "There's Michael Jordan and then there's the rest of us."

So, what records does Michael Jordan actually hold in career statistics? A lot of people think he must be the most prolific scorer in NBA history, number one in percentage of field goals, or has scored the most points in a single game. *Think again!* Michael Jordan isn't the greatest scorer. He doesn't have the highest field goal percentage, and he's not even the greatest rebounder. In fact, he holds only one top NBA statistic. Michael Jordan has missed more shots than anyone else.

What, then, constitutes his greatness? Could it be in part the fact that he has risked failure more often than anyone else? What if he'd passed on the winning shot in 1998 against the Utah Jazz to win the NBA title? Or hadn't attempted that last-second shot to beat Phoenix in 1993? If he hadn't risked failure by taking those shots, his legendary status would be somewhat diminished.

Here's what we can learn from Michael Jordan. If you seek big possibilities, you have to risk big failures. Some pursue their possibilities only up to the point where they begin to encounter discouragement. Then they choose retreat.

If you can honestly say, "I've never been discouraged," then I suspect you have sidestepped possibilities. If you believe that your path to possibilities means avoiding mistakes and missteps, you're depriving yourself of life's true richness. Have you ever heard of someone sleeping on the floor because they are don't want to risk falling out of bed? It seems they settle for the discomfort of the floor because they are "certain" they will not fall! Possibility producers take the top bunk!

There is a popular saying tennis coaches use to inspire players to take risk. "You miss 100 percent of the shots you do not take!" Don't be afraid to risk some failures on the way to achieving extraordinary possibilities.

BE AN AMATEUR

Suppose you were about to have surgery and the nurse said, "Don't worry–your doctor is an amateur." Or your plane was in a fierce storm and the flight attendant tried to comfort you with, "Relax–the pilot is a real amateur." How would you feel?

You might be tempted to leap out of the hospital bed or even parachute out of the plane. To many, the word "amateur" means someone inexperienced, unprofessional, or unskilled–even someone who is definitely going to make a botch of what they do. But *think again!*

"Amateur" comes from the Latin word for love and is defined as "one who loves or has a taste for anything." When you decide to convert "impossible" to "possible," you start by falling passionately in love with what you want to achieve, and you become a true "amateur."

Lackadaisical or halfhearted just isn't going to hack it. If you reluctantly feel you really *ought* to be doing something, or you believe something *might* be fun or useful if you tried it, what kind of fierce ingenuity and fiery energy are you likely to come up with? If your goal and passion aren't in total alignment, you're just going to spin your wheels and overlook your many possibilities.

What keeps you up at night? This statement is frequently used to identify problems, individually and organizationally. A typical response is, "I'll tell you what keeps me up–*stress!*"

What about taking the thoughts of all the things that generate stress and replacing them with thoughts of success instead? How about using this mindset to quantify your possibilities or ambitions?

Certainly life's challenges can cause restless nights, but have you ever been kept awake by a potential possibility you are pursuing? That indicates you are tapping into your passions. If you are so full of anticipation for the next day or next opportunity that it keeps you awake at night, then you are becoming a true "amateur." You're shifting your focus from the uneasiness of worry to the exhilaration of possibilities.

> *Schedule a "heart scan."* Follow your heart and intuition. Life is short. Don't waste it in pursuit of someone else's dreams. Don't let others' limited perspectives prevent you from achieving abundant possibilities. Avoid people who resist the notion of amateur and want you to do the "right" or the practical thing. This does not require a professional opinion. As an "amateur," you are your own best "heart specialist."

> *Show me the money.* A clear indication that you are becoming an "amateur" is answering "yes" to questions like, "Would I do this for free?" or "Would I even pay for the pleasure of doing it?" When you plug into your passions, money becomes secondary to meaning. Purpose is preeminent over power.

You may have heard the phrase, "Do what you love and the money will follow." A true "amateur" says, "If I do what I love, joy and contentment will follow." Money has importance, but it never replaces the value of things that energize our hearts and souls.

DARE TO GIVE UP

There's a popular theory that if you do ten things well and one thing badly, you must concentrate all your time and energy on improving that single deficiency. *Think again!*

Of *course* we might benefit by single-mindedly pursuing perfection in an area we feel inadequate. But time and energy are not infinite. If you make a good faith effort and fail miserably at a single aspect of your project, quantify your progress by asking yourself these questions:

- Can I overcome this deficiency if I try hard enough?

- Must this shortcoming keep me from achieving my goal?

- Could others be harmed if I don't have this particular skill?

If you can honestly answer "no" to these questions, move on to new possibilities. You have my permission to stop beating yourself up over what you do badly and concentrate on what you do *well.* Build on your strengths! Either devise a strategy that eliminates the need for this talent from your project, or subcontract this aspect out to someone else. You can consciously decide that your precious resources would be better devoted to what you are *good* at—to what you're *passionate* about—and move on toward your goal.

One necessary element of realizing great possibilities is to get great at knowing what you're truly *bad* at. We can each do almost anything in life. But we can't do *everything* in life. I learned this life lesson recently at a speaking engagement in Bermuda. An activity was planned in which the attendees would hop onto motor scooters and tour the island. An exhilarating excursion, to be sure, but I got caught up in the excitement and neglected to evaluate my strengths and weaknesses for this activity.

I was so engrossed in anticipation that I overlooked the fact that, with my hands shaped as they are and having limited dexterity, applying the hand brakes on a motor scooter would be challenging—okay, *impossible*. I hopped onto my scooter like everyone else and hit the gas. *Then* I realized that I wouldn't be able to stop! I had to circle the parking lot for several minutes until a speedy hotel employee caught up to me and brought me to a halt. An ignominious but safe conclusion to an endeavor I should not have started. But by daring to give up, I had saved myself a great deal of grief and the tour organizers the cost of a new scooter.

When you quantify your progress and revaluate your potential remember, never let what you cannot do get in the way of what you can do!

Everybody has talent; it's just a matter of moving around until you've discovered what it is.

— GEORGE LUCAS
AWARD-WINNING PRODUCER,
DIRECTOR, SCREENWRITER

DREAM THE IMPOSSIBLE DREAM

Who can think of the words, "To dream the impossible dream..." without hearing the incomparable Robert Goulet belting out the theme from Man of La Mancha? I think we take to heart the commitment of Don Quixote, and we want to follow our own quest, "No matter how hopeless, no matter how far."

The problem is, most of us think our own struggles with everyday life are in the same category as trying to bring peace to the Middle East. We place too much importance on most decisions, agonizing over them endlessly, and not enough on the few genuine, life-changing choices we can make.

If we really distill our life choices, there are only three important questions that define our lives:

- Where do I make my home?

- With whom do I share my life?

- What is possible for me?

Can you think of any other questions that have a greater impact on your life?

Here's an exciting thought, one that fuels my passion about possibilities: *possibilities have never been so abundant.*

We are living in perhaps the greatest era of opportunity the world has ever known. There has never before been a time and a place in which individuals hold so many possibilities in their hands. Think of the myriad of options, knowledge, decisions, and alternatives available to *you*.

The explosion of technology has opened doors to possibilities that just a short time ago would have been impossible. Years ago, the ability to explore possibilities was nearly always limited. You could spend your entire life in the place where you were born. Your profession was determined by what your family had done before you, and your elders preselected your life partner. Your contact with others could have been limited to your tribe or village.

All these limitations are still true for many people throughout the world, but if you are reading this book, it is probably not true for *you!* I hope you now have a new appreciation of how much is available to you, once you begin to notice, evaluate, choose, and pursue *your world of possibilities*.

Each of us has a purpose in life, a passion we were created to pursue. I hope this book has inspired you, through its true stories and bits of wisdom, to look for opportunities of impossible possibilities. I end with lyrics that capture the essence of possibility thinking. May you follow the exciting path available to you as you *think again* and enjoy the quest for an abundant life.

THE IMPOSSIBLE DREAM

Lyrics by Joe Darien

To dream... the impossible dream...
To fight... the unbeatable foe...
To bear... with unbearable sorrow...
To run... where the brave dare not go...
To right... the unrightable wrong...
To love... pure and chaste from afar...
To try... when your arms are too weary...
To reach... the unreachable star...

This is my quest, to follow that star...
No matter how hopeless, no matter how far...
To fight for the right, without question or pause...
To be willing to march into Hell,
for a Heavenly cause...

And I know if I'll only be true, to this glorious quest,
That my heart will lie will lie peaceful and calm,
when I'm laid to my rest...
And the world will be better for this:
That one man, scorned and covered with scars,
Still strove, with his last ounce of courage,
To reach... the unreachable star...

INDEX

Adragna, Dan 63

Agassi, Andre 165

Alessandra, Tony 217

Anderson, Fred 181

Anderson, Pat 181

Aquinas, Saint Thomas 144

Arlen, Harold 45

Baker, Nancy 11

Baldacci, David 140

Baldwin, James A. 47

Baltimore Orioles 101

Berra, Yogi 47

Bombeck, Erma 115

Brinkley, David 155

Burke, James 140

California Future Farmers of
America 123

Canfield, Jack 16

Carlson, Richard 73

Casals, Pablo 182

Chicken Soup for the Soul 16

Chick the Singing Pig 169

Churchill, Winston 141

Clarke, Arthur C. 39

Cleveland Rotary Club 158

Cleveland Terminal Tower 158

Coolidge, Calvin 209

Cosby, Bill 211

Coward, Noël 114

Crawford, Alexa 11, 69, 125, 199

Crawford, Kathryn 83, 119, 121

DePree, Max 159

Dickinson, Emily 89

Dick Van Dyke Show 43

Dinesen, Isak 204

Don't Sweat the Small Stuff 73

Edison, Thomas 79

Einstein, Albert 137

Emerson, Ralph Waldo 118

Failing Forward 170

Ford, Henry 163

framing 154

Fresno Convention Center 123

Fuldheim, Dorothy 203

Goldwyn, Samuel 21

Grace, Nancy 12

Grameen Bank 161

Great America 64

Greenbrook Racquet Club 61

Griffith, Melanie 140

Grimes, Bob 143

Hammarsjöld, Dag 208

Harris, Thomas A. 106

Hastings, Reed 33

Hempfing, Phil 101

Hill, Christopher 125

Hill, Monica 119, 125

Hill, Napoleon 218

Hornbuckle, Bill 166

How High Can You Bounce? 82, 189, 194

Jackson, Mahalia 177

Jason, Harvey 29

Jobs, Steve 88

Johnson, Gary 133

Johnson, Magic 219

Johnson, Samuel 124

Jordan, Michael 219

Kaiser, Henry J. 66

Kay-Shuttleworth, Rachel 186

Keller, Helen 139, 198

Kennedy, John F. 110

King, Larry 11

Knowles, Eleanor 143

Leighton, Mrs. 119

Link, Henry C. 206

Loyola Marymount University 12, 62

Lucas, George 226

Lucchetti, Dave 179

Martin, Dave 97

Maxwell, John 170

McEnroe, John 12

Mercer, Johnny 45

Microcredit Summit 162

Miller, Jim 179

Milne, A.A. 71

Morduch, Jonathan J. 161

Mystery Pier Books 29

National Skeet Shooting Hall of Fame 57

Navratilova, Martina 173

NCAA 62

Netflix 33

Olivier, Laurence 77

Orlando Magic 169

Ornish, Dr. Dean 175

Orwell, George 49

Pabco Gypsum 179

Pacific Coast Building Products 179

Paige, Leroy (Satchel) 213

Parker, Roy 166

Pasteur, Louis 102

Patton, George S. 75

Peale, Dr. Norman Vincent 30

Pee-wee's Big Adventure 43

Philadelphia 76ers 169

Pride Industries 171

Purpose-Driven Life, The 24

Qubein, Nido 206
Redmoon, Ambrose 196
Ripken, Cal 101
Robert, Cavett 205
Rowling, J.K. 29, 32
Salz, Jeff 70
Sculley, John 88
Shakespeare, William 106
Sims, David B.P. 154
Souza, Alfred D. 192
Spielberg, Steven 29
Stevenson, Adlai 51
Sullivan, Anne 139
Thoreau, Henry David 152
Thornton, Tony 143
thought-interruption 81
Twain, Mark 196
United States Professional Tennis
    Association 12, 62
Walter Reed Army Medical Center
    193
Warren, Rick 24
Washington, D.C. 140, 162, 193
Wayne, John 196
Wheels for the World 65
Williams, Pat 169
Williamson, Marianne 127
Winnie-the-Pooh 71
Woods, Harry 143
Working Girl 140
Yogananda, Paramahansa 200

Young, Judy Allen 57
Yunus, Muhammad 161
Ziegler, Michael 171
Zoom Imaging Solutions 133